A GIFT FOR THE FUTURE

Conversations About Estate Planning

LINDSEY PAIGE MARKUS, J.D., M.A.

Ida Rose Publishing, LLC
Lindsey Paige Markus, M.A., J.D.
120 S. Riverside Plaza, Suite 1700 | Chicago, IL 60606
www.AGiftForTheFuture.com

ISBN: 978-0-578-32508-8

To my clients.
Past, present and future.

Many years ago, I walked away from a lucrative career in finance because I wanted to make more of a difference in people's lives. I hope I've made a difference in yours. There has never been a day since when I've doubted the path I chose. But there are certain days when I can actually see how we've helped a client's family, including future generations, live their best life. Days when we see a grandchild graduate college debt-free because of a grandmother's bequest. Days when an estate is distributed exactly according to a client's wishes, despite a complicated family situation. Days when a charity receives a large bequest from a donor who wanted to leave a lasting legacy in the community long after their death. Days when a wife can mourn a beloved husband without worrying about losing her home, accessing funds or providing for her family.

There have been so many days like these and more. These are the days I cherish the most and the reason I wrote this book.

Disclaimers

Legislative Updates

Estate tax and income tax laws constantly change. While the legislative landscape remains in flux, the need to engage in dynamic estate planning is more critical than ever. For updates on tax legislation as it impacts *A Gift for the Future*, please visit www.AGiftfortheFuture.com/legalupdates.

Legal

This publication does not constitute or create an attorney-client relationship between Lindsey Paige Markus and a reader. We have made every attempt to ensure the information contained herein is accurate; however, Lindsey Paige Markus and Ida Rose Publishing, LLC are not responsible for any errors, omissions or results obtained from the use of the information contained herein. The information contained herein is intended for a general overview and discussion of estate planning and wealth protection and is not intended as a substitute for engaging a licensed attorney to work with you and your family to craft an estate plan to meet your specific needs.

Foreword

By Russell W. Sullivan

In late 2010 (and again in 2012), President Obama and congressional Democrats faced difficult tax policy decisions. The tax cuts created by the Economic Growth and Tax Reconciliation Relief Act of 2001 (EGTRRA) were set to expire in 2011. Progressive Democrats wanted many of the tax cuts to terminate, while moderates preferred that only some be extended and others be modified before being made permanent.

At the time, I was honored to be serving as staff director of the Senate Finance Committee for the Democrats. Our party held a slight majority in the Senate but not the sufficient supermajority required to pass legislation without Republican support. The estate tax was at the center of Senate debate — especially in 2010. A majority of Democrats opposed the full repeal of the estate tax, which was set to take effect on January 1, 2010, under EGTRRA. Across the aisle, most Republicans voiced concern over the proposed sidecar provision that would have repealed step-up in basis. Negotiations ensued.

Senator Jon Kyl (R-AZ) and Senator Blanche Lincoln (D-AK) led the group of negotiators seeking the broadest possible relief that could pass the Senate. Other Democrats urged returning to a low exemption amount and high estate tax rate. My boss at the time, Chairman Max Baucus (D-MT), and Finance Committee ranking member Chuck Grassley (R-IA) worked with Senators Kyl and Lincoln on a compromise.

During negotiations, I turned to a group of Chicago-based estate and gift tax attorneys for advice. Lindsey Paige Markus was a key leader of that group, and I trusted her expertise and advice, as she had educated me through the years on a wide range of business and wealth management issues surrounding the estate tax. I traveled to Chicago at least once a year to speak with these attorneys, accountants, trust advisors and asset managers. Lindsey grounded these legislative proposals in real-world examples. I was consistently amazed by her intellect, and I grew to trust her judgment on all manner of estate tax issues.

You may or may not support the compromise agreed to in 2010. We can argue whether a $5 million exemption amount and 40% rate was the right policy or even whether the U.S. should have an estate tax at all. What is not up for debate in my mind is that Lindsey is one of the great tax minds in this field. Her experience and practical estate planning expertise proved invaluable in crafting a compromise that ultimately raised the estate exemption amount above pre-EGTTRA levels and protected the stepped-up basis. In the years that followed, legislators continued to propose tax increases on the estate transfer process, and through it all, Lindsey has remained a strong advocate for estate planners across the country.

The conversation around estate transfer taxation began to heat up again in 2020. As the presidential election started to take shape, several progressive policymakers introduced proposals to increase taxes on entrepreneurs who had succeeded in creating wealth. Democratic candidates highlighted data illustrating a record-high concentration of wealth in the hands of a few citizens and suggested various approaches to taxing the wealth earned by these risk-takers. Senator Elizabeth Warren (D-MA) recommended an annual 2% tax on assets held by millionaires; Senator Bernie Sanders (D-VT) proposed a 77% estate tax rate. In his first proposed budget, President Joe Biden suggested that death should be a taxable event that would trigger both capital gains and estate taxes. He also proposed a repeal of the step-up in basis for the heir. Although none of these proposals passed in 2022, lawmakers will continue to advocate for taxes on wealth in their efforts to reduce income inequality.

Perhaps the boldest proposal was introduced by Senator Ron Wyden (D-OR) to tax wealth like wages. The proposal would impose capital gains taxes on personal assets each year, regardless of whether the assets were sold or not. This annual mark-to-market for individually-owned assets eliminates the recognition principle that had long served as a foundation of U.S. federal tax laws. Senator Wyden's dramatic proposal may not succeed in the short run, but the creativity of policymakers seeking to tax wealth will expand and spread to state legislatures seeking similar goals.

Current policy trends make it more critical than ever to master the options available for individuals to protect their assets. Lindsey shows us how to do so.

A Gift for the Future is an excellent, in-depth guide for estate planning with the current tax code. With clever real-world examples designed to keep any reader engaged, Lindsey explains estate and income taxes, lifetime exemptions, business structures, and various types of trusts and estate planning tools, along with explanations on how to use them to maximize the legacy you leave to your loved ones and charitable organizations.

It is a well-organized guide to walk readers through individual life situations — single parents, married couples, blended families, divorcees — in a choose-your-own-adventure type format. Throughout the book, Lindsey shows the reader how to get started and explains how to compassionately engage in some of these difficult conversations, all in a readable style.

Death and taxes are inevitable for all of us, making this book a wonderful tool for everyone. And Lindsey's ability to help guide readers through complex estate planning techniques makes this a must read for high-net-worth individuals. Lindsey's thoughtful attention to family dynamics with a personalized touch makes it clear how her extraordinary bedside manner makes a stay-at-home spouse feel heard and protected, as it does for high-net-worth individuals who entrust her with creating a legacy for multiple generations and philanthropic organizations.

The guide also proves to be a valuable resource for practitioners in complementary disciplines — accountants, insurance brokers and wealth advisors — looking to piece together various planning techniques.

Reciting the tax code by number alone is not an indication of mastery. Lindsey, however, does demonstrate mastery of the subject in *A Gift for the Future* by her outstanding ability to interpret the code, explain it effectively and apply it in a way to help others. She has advised thousands of families and business owners across the country on estate and succession planning.

Throughout her career she has made it her mission to educate others through speaking and writing — and now her book, *A Gift for the Future*, is an outgrowth of that mission. It provides a well-written roadmap for the complex journey through the terrain of death and taxes.

Russell Sullivan is a shareholder at Brownstein Hyatt Farber Schreck in Washington D.C. He served on the Senate Finance Committee for 14 years as chief tax counsel and as staff director. During that time he played a major role in crafting important tax legislation, including 2001 and 2003 tax cut bills, 2004 domestic jobs bill, 2007 energy policy act and the milestone Affordable Care Act.

TABLE OF CONTENTS

PREFACE

My mother and father are both doctors, Dad, a successful surgeon, and Mom, a renowned neuro-cognitive therapist, putting them in the upper 2% in terms of educational achievement. They are smart and successful people, but not members of the 1% club, those fabulously rich families many people think are the only ones who need estate planning. Yet they do need an estate plan, and they had a sense that a prior plan may not have been enough. If two brilliant doctors needed an education about estate planning, how can we expect the rest of us to know how a good estate plan works?

When my father first showed me their estate plan, my initial reaction was to blurt out: "Dad, where's the rest?" It was my first year of practice and he wanted me to review it, but the short stack of papers in his hand told me much was missing. My father also handed me a stack of articles he had collected on estate planning, so he knew they needed a more comprehensive plan but simply didn't know where or how to begin the process.

My parents and I sat down together and started a conversation.

They had a basic will, but they had never had a conversation with their attorney about the many valuable estate planning tools available to them. They never talked about how a simple revocable living trust could dramatically minimize the taxes their estate would owe, help avoid the vagaries of probate court, and protect assets for their beneficiaries. Consequently, my parents' plan did little to minimize state estate taxes or protect their estate from potential creditors — a constant worry for any medical professional. I remember thinking that if this could happen to two such smart and benevolent people, it could happen to anyone.

After helping my parents with their estate plan, I made it my mission to teach people about estate planning. Early in my career, I launched www.lindseymarkus.com to share estate planning education with others, and this book is the next step in ensuring that people understand why and how they can benefit from estate planning. To me, teaching is a good deed. I truly believe that if you do something good and teach someone something, the universe will give you something back. Who couldn't use some good karma?

The desire to help others has always been part of who I am, but my path to estate planning educator and attorney was a bit unconventional. When deciding on college majors, I was torn between drama and economics. The two could not have been more different. I ultimately went into international economics and finance because I found it more intellectually challenging. But after a few successful stints traveling the globe and structuring international business deals, two things became clear. First, I didn't have a passion for what I was doing because I wasn't helping people directly and, second, there was an attorney present at every critical juncture in my career. That's when I decided to go to law school, though I had no idea where it would take me. By my second year of law school it became clear that I wanted to make a difference in the lives of others through estate planning.

Why estate planning? Because it's a people business. I meet daily with families from all walks of life. Some estates are more complex than others, but everyone has the desire to see their life's work protected and passed on in a specific way. The process requires people to get metaphorically naked. They have to open their books, tell me who they love and who they don't, and share their vision and hopes for their family. This intimate process is special to me because they are trusting me with their most tightly held concerns. Studies have repeatedly shown that people would prefer to talk about almost anything more than their money. Sex, drug addiction and marital issues are all easier to talk about than money. Since people are at their most vulnerable when discussing their finances, it is my job to ensure their trust in me and that the well-being of their family is handled with the same depth of seriousness and concern. Some people want to make sure their surviving spouse is well cared for. Others want to make sure their children get as large an inheritance as possible, and perhaps protect them from themselves. Still others want to fund favored charities, care for relatives with special needs or fund their grandchildren's education. Some family trees are complex, with different branches formed after divorce or death. Every estate plan is a puzzle, and I enjoy helping people put the pieces in the right places.

Although many people think estate planning is only for the wealthy, the opposite is actually true. Virtually everyone who cares about how their life's work lives on after they are gone can benefit from good estate planning. If you've ever seen how probate costs can eat into the assets a person leaves behind, or how an unforeseen lawsuit can deplete a child's inheritance, you know the importance of good estate planning.

Although many people think estate planning is only for the wealthy, the opposite is actually true

Estate planning is not an abstraction or a matter of preparing forms. The words tell a personal story. The purpose and meaning in what I do comes from getting to truly know my clients and understanding what they want their family legacy to be. While the product delivered may be a stack of legal documents like those my parents now have, those papers are about caring for the people named within. I ask all my clients for a family photo to ensure that we remember who we're working for — the smiling kids and the happy parents. The family photo serves as a constant reminder of why a well-planned estate is truly a gift for the future.

INTRODUCTION

With all the things going on in your life, why should you spend time reading about a subject as dry as estate planning? Possibly because you care about the people you may someday leave behind. I have helped hundreds of individuals and their families plan their estates. Every client has greatly enriched my life because of the joy they felt knowing their family will be cared for and their life's work will be protected and distributed exactly according to their wishes. If you could see the look in a man's eyes who just realized he no longer has to fear what will happen to his disabled daughter after he is gone, you would know that estate planning is not a dry science. Estate planning plays such a valuable role in a family's life; it will live on long after death. Peace of mind is a powerful gift.

Who is This Book Written For?

Everyone. Throughout this book there are examples related to married couples and their kids. While these types of families make up the majority of American households, they are not the only ones who need estate planning. It's just as imperative for single individuals, married couples with no children, for people in non-married, committed relationships and for people who are single parents by choice or circumstance. Virtually all of the planning ideas discussed will work for the family you created.

Estate planning is not just for wealthy people either. Certainly, if you've had great financial success, you will want to ensure your estate doesn't get cut in half by federal and state estate taxes after you are gone. However, tax minimization is just one function of a good estate plan.

Today, the average size of an inheritance in America is almost $180,000. Yet, in some states, any estate in excess of $15,000 is in danger of being diluted by probate costs. Estates can also be distributed by the state in ways you may not have wanted and subject to seizure by creditors. This happens when individuals do not develop good estate plans during their life. Nothing good happens without a plan. But, where to start?

Every Good Estate Plan Begins with a Conversation

The starting point for a good estate plan is understanding how you want your assets to be used, and by whom, after you die. It is also helpful to understand the estate planning tools available to fulfill your wishes. Talking with your family and loved ones can help you decide what you want to happen when you're gone, and it also ensures that they know your wishes. An open conversation with an estate planning attorney can put the plans in place to make your wishes a reality while reducing taxes owed and protecting assets for your beneficiaries. Although these may be difficult conversations, keep in mind they are actually a gift to your loved ones.

With proper planning, your heirs' stress and work will be reduced

After you're gone, an estate planning attorney will deal with the living on your behalf. With proper planning, your heirs' stress and work will be reduced, allowing them to focus on healing and moving forward rather than court dates and judges' rulings.

Arguably, people with a larger net worth need to take even

more care with estate planning to preserve assets for intended beneficiaries, instead of being diluted by estate taxes, attorney fees and the court system. But even modest estates contain the seeds of destruction.

Louise was a single woman with no children. She managed to save about $225,000 from her long career as a factory worker. She wanted to split the money among her five great-nieces and great-nephews, but her estate was poorly planned. After her death, a long-lost brother, who hadn't communicated with the family for over 40 years, suddenly reappeared and managed to take a big chunk out of the estate leaving hard feelings and legal bills for other family members to deal with. This did not have to happen.

A well-done estate plan is the perfect addendum to a life well lived.

A Time to Look Forward and Backward

Planning your estate is a time to reflect on the things most important to you. What have you built? What's important to you? What do you want your legacy to be? This is a moment in life ripe with both meaning and possibilities. Many people spend their entire life looking forward, working to get ahead. When you sit down with an estate planning professional, it is time to think about what all your efforts have gotten you and your family. It is also a time to think about how you'd like to be taken care of in your twilight years.

Chapter 1 looks at the basic documents most people need. These are tools used to fulfill your wishes. How these tools are wielded depends on your passions and desires.

Before any plan is put into place though, there are some things you need to consider in the event of a life-altering incapacitation or death.

1. **Who do you trust to look after children?**
   For many people, the impetus to do estate planning is triggered by a growing family and desire to identify guardians to care for your children. The person or person(s) you identify to raise the children may be different from who you trust to look after the funds.

2. **Who do you trust to handle your affairs upon your death or if you are incapacitated?**
   There may well come a time when you no longer want to or are incapable of handling financial and property-related matters. An estate plan identifies the individual you trust to make decisions not only upon your death, but also in the event of your incapacity. You can give someone a power of attorney for property (or durable power of attorney) to act on your behalf over assets held in your individual name. The name is misleading because it doesn't only apply to property decisions, it covers all financial decisions. In estate plans that include a revocable living trust (discussed in the first chapter), a successor trustee or decision maker is identified to act over assets held in the name of your trust. Typically, whoever you trust to make administrative or financial decisions is also appointed to carry out your wishes upon death.

3. **How do you want healthcare-related decisions made?**
   A power of attorney for healthcare (often called an advance directive for health care), or living will, detailing how you want health care decisions to be handled is important for anyone over age 18 and especially for those dealing with

end-of-life issues. Is quality of life important to you if you became very ill or were in an accident? Have you considered organ donation? It's a good idea to make these decisions for yourself before you are no longer able to provide guidance.

4. Who do you want to take care of after your death?

If you keep your estate out of probate, there are no hard and fast rules concerning who can benefit from your life's work. Are there people beyond your family you would like to bequeath part of your estate? Do certain family members need more help than others? Do you have treasured assets that may have more meaning to some family members or friends than others? Are there some family members who cannot be trusted to immediately inherit a large sum of money?

Sometimes things are complicated. There may be distant family members you feel certain will challenge your estate decisions. There may be exes and family of exes whom you may want to include or definitely exclude. There are no right or wrong answers or moral judgments when it comes to family dynamics. It's up to you to decide how your estate can do the most good for family members and others you have cherished in your life.

5. Do you want to leave a philanthropic legacy?

During your life you may have, or will become, very close to charities and organizations that benefit others. You may have a passion for art, children or mental health. There may be a disease you would like to help eradicate or a favored sport you would like to see made available for those less fortunate. There may be a university or school that has been important in your life or that offers a special program that interests you. There may be a friend, relative or mentor you would like to honor. Perhaps there is some other good you would like to do for others. The list of good things you can do with any amount of money is endless. This is a good time to think about your passions in life and whether you'd like part of your estate to leave a legacy.

6. What do you want to happen with your business?
If you own an interest in a business, knowing what you want to happen to that business will go a long way toward determining how future ownership and management is structured. How your wishes are executed may also determine whether the business continues to have a prosperous future.

Keep Your Plan Up to Date

There is one facet of estate planning often overlooked by even the most diligent people. Laws change as do family situations and circumstances. If you don't regularly update your estate plan, the best-laid plans can go awry if they aren't updated to comport with tax and legislative changes.

Bob and Pam had an estate plan in place that was not updated when state tax laws changed. When Bob passed away, Pam was surprised to learn that more than $1 million was owed to the state; money that she surely could have put to better use.

In another instance, Judy had two children, a son and a daughter, and her intention was to leave everything to them to be split 50-50. Unfortunately, she added her daughter to the title of her house and on her bank account thinking she was making things easier on her loved ones. However, she didn't account for a falling-out between her children, nor did she alter her plan when the falling-out occurred. In the end, those assets legally passed only to her daughter.

Hard-earned money can do so much good in this world, but it does tend to bring out the worst in some people. Again, with proper estate planning, you can control how the estate you spent a lifetime building is used after you are gone.

Why People Wait Too Long

Some time ago I was talking to Carl Jerome of the North Shore Meditation and Dharma Center, whom I respectfully refer to as "my Buddha." We discussed why some people put off getting their estate plans in order, and he offered two succinct observations.

"Most people simply don't realize that it is more comfortable and peaceful to have a well-organized estate plan now than to put it off"

"One [reason] is the sense we all have of being permanent," he said. "The way our minds process information, there appears to be a permanent self. As my mother who's well into her 90s jokingly says, 'You're never going to get rid of me; I'm going to live forever.'"

I suspect this is the attitude most at play when celebrities, like Prince, die without a will or prior estate planning in place. Everyone jokes about the only certainties in life being death and taxes, but most don't like to discuss it.

The other reason Carl mentioned was a bit more subtle: "Most people simply don't realize that it is more comfortable and peaceful to have a well-organized estate plan now than to put it off."

It has long been known there are mental health benefits to leading an orderly life. Time and again individuals are surprised by the sense of empowerment and peace they feel having a plan in place. However, I wonder if more people shouldn't consider the chaos likely to occur when a person of means dies without having taken the time to do an estate plan. Ask the loved ones Prince left behind.

Certainly Prince died prematurely, but those things happen. A few years later, his heirs, potential heirs and wanna-be heirs were still fighting acrimonious battles in court. Millions of fans may worship his music, but those he loved the most were left with a mess to clean up and significant estate taxes. Most surprising to me was that, as a young artist, Prince delayed signing recording contracts because he wanted to make certain he retained artistic license and control. A master planner in many ways, he failed to address his own mortality. As one of the first artists to support AIDS philanthropy and education, had a plan been in place, his estate could have helped fund a cure. Instead, hundreds of millions of dollars went to Uncle Sam to pay estate taxes.

This happens all the time. According to data compiled by *Forbes Magazine*, 54% of Americans aged 55 to 64 do not have a will. Those people are in danger of having their estates fund legal battles rather than comfortable lives for their loved ones.

The Gift That Keeps on Giving

If you postpone or fail to update your estate plan, the repercussions can be severe. While all of this will be covered in more depth throughout this book, the following can be serious blows to your intended wishes:

- **Taxes.** A huge tax bite can dramatically shrink estates built up over a lifetime or even generations. Estate tax liabilities can be as high as 50%. When most people think of estate taxes, they worry about the dreaded federal tax on estates. Under the current law, in 2022, the federal estate tax only affects those estates larger than $12.06 million, or $24.12 million for a married couple. Many don't realize that the high exemptions are only in effect until the end of 2025 and, in 2026, they will be cut in half. However, for people who reside in a state with a separate estate tax exemption, estate tax liabilities arise at amounts as low as $1 million. Actually, state thresholds vary drastically and are discussed more in Chapter 16 and throughout this book. With the current estate tax exemption so high, the larger threat for many people relates to income taxes. But with proper planning, income tax liabilities and estate tax liabilities at the federal and state level can be managed, minimized and sometimes completely avoided.

- **Court Administration.** Poorly planned estates end up in probate court — the judicial process of administering an estate, which is expensive, time-consuming and a matter of public record. Again, the threshold to avoid probate can be as low as $15,000 in some states. Just like state tax thresholds, these amounts vary dramatically and are covered more in depth in Chapter 16. With probate, a judge oversees the estate administration, requiring notice to creditors and court appearances that create tremendous inefficiencies. Your wishes play a secondary role to a judge's interpretation of the law and your family situation. And when assets pass to a minor child, you run the risk of having to open a guardian estate for each child and report to the court annually as to how the funds are used. Little good happens when probate is in control.

- **Creditor Exposure.** Failure to plan can put inheritance intended for a surviving spouse or child in the hands of a creditor — whether they are a typical creditor or one resulting from a malpractice claim or an ex-spouse trying to make a claim for maintenance or alimony.

- **Lost Legacy.** Without a plan, you lose the opportunity to leave a legacy. You may feel passionate about providing educational funds for grandchildren or perhaps there is a charity that you would like to leave a lasting benefit to. Without proper estate planning, people and organizations you care about will be left with nothing from you.

For all the chaos and unfulfilled opportunities left behind by those who don't carefully plan their estates, there are an equal number of opportunities that grow from proper estate planning.

Estate Planning is Your Link to the Future

Most people spend their lives trying to accomplish something. Perhaps it's becoming a successful business person, an admired professional, a loved mother or father, a mentor or a friend. Whatever you've done or will do with your life will be reflected in what you leave behind. After you're gone, a good estate plan ensures that your life's work does the things you want it to do.

The role of an estate planning attorney is to make sure your wishes are executed so that your life's work does not result in chaos after you pass. The ones you love, the passions you've enjoyed and the assets you've built can be well-taken care of when you are gone. This book, along with the help of a qualified estate planning attorney, will guide you through the conversations you need to have to ensure that you have organized your thoughts and wishes and considered the possible eventualities, which in the end, is a gift for the future.

SECTION 1:

Foundations of Estate Planning

Estate planning attorneys use a variety of tools to help you leave a well-planned estate — an estate plan that takes care of those you want taken care of and maximizes the value of the assets you leave behind. However, it is your money, it is your family, they are your dreams and it is your estate plan. The more you know, the better job your attorney can do. So let's look at a few of the basics you should understand before we get started.

Chapter 1
Basics of Estate Planning

You have to understand what an estate plan is and what life events trigger the need to put one together or update an existing plan. At the most basic level, an estate plan is a way to distribute your assets upon your death. Often people think they need a will to say who gets what when they are gone. But a will is only one of the basic tools you can use, and a will alone does not allow you to avoid the court system. How this is done takes careful planning. That's where you can truly benefit from the help of a professional. With an understanding of what goes into an estate plan, you will be prepared for those conversations you will have with your estate planning attorney and loved ones throughout the process.

Guiding Principles of Estate Planning

There are three principles which guide estate planning:
- Minimize taxes
- Avoid the courts
- Layer in asset protection

— *Tax minimization*

Historically, the focus on tax minimization was always directed at estate taxes, primarily because the estate tax can be as high as 50% for every dollar over the exemption or tax-free amount. Proper estate planning can help to ensure that tax exemptions are leveraged. And now that the estate tax exemption has increased dramatically ($12.06 million at the federal level in 2022) for clients without concerns about estate taxes, the focus has shifted from estate taxes to income taxes.

The estate and income tax analysis can send you into a whirlwind. For those interested in learning more, Chapter 2 provides a more detailed explanation. For those not particularly interested in the tax planning mechanisms, feel free to skim that chapter.

— *Avoid the courts*

Although the threshold to avoid taxes is currently high, the threshold to avoid the court system at death, known as probate, can be as low as $15,000. Thus, while tax planning may not be applicable to all clients, everyone needs to avoid the probate system. And, for those with minor children, it is also critical to avoid guardian estates for minors. This is the primary reason a "basic will" alone is not enough. Even with a well-drafted will if, upon my death, I own assets in my individual name that total more than the probate threshold ($100,000 in Illinois), my family would have to go through the lengthy process of probate to reach the assets.

Layer in Asset Protection

Many think that a basic estate plan will provide asset protection from creditors. In reality, only a few states offer creditor protection over assets owned during your lifetime. But all clients are eager to ensure that the assets left to loved ones go to loved ones and not to a creditor. By adding asset protection tools to your estate plan, you will ensure assets end up where you intended.

Who Do You Trust?

Some are fearful that estate planning means that they will lose control over their assets. In reality, you can continue to retain total control over your finances by identifying someone who can act in the event of your incapacity or upon your death.

It's also a time to ask yourself, who do you trust to handle the following roles?

- **Executor:** You will need to name an executor (or personal representative) to work with probate and make sure the wishes expressed in your will are followed as closely as possible. The executor will also be responsible for safeguarding assets while your probate estate is being settled.

- **Guardian:** Who do you trust with guardianship of your children's futures if you and your spouse die unexpectedly in a car accident? Who should care for disabled or special needs dependents? A guardian, or team of guardians, will care for your children on an ongoing basis.

- **Trustee for Finances:** You will need to name the person you want to manage assets you put in trust. In the event of your incapacity, the successor trustee manages assets that were transferred to your trust on your behalf. Upon your death, the successor trustee works with the executor (often the same person) to pay any taxes, and he or she is charged with carrying out the wishes of your trust. Often this means looking after the trust assets for beneficiaries and determining how and when distributions will be made until a beneficiary is old enough to manage the trust assets for themselves.

- **Powers of Attorney:** Whom do you trust with extraordinary powers to make healthcare and financial decisions on your behalf? You can also create a **springing power of attorney** that only goes into effect if you become incapacitated.

As you will see, an estate planning attorney tries to look at every eventuality and document how you want things handled "in the event of ...." These are not decisions you want to make on the spur of the moment or while sitting in a lengthy estate planning meeting.

These are not decisions you want to make on the spur of the moment

How Assets Are Distributed

When planning your estate, keep in mind how the things you own or control are passed to others who are called beneficiaries. Basically, there are several ways your assets can be dispersed:

- **By Will.** The most basic estate planning tool details how you want everything you own distributed and to whom. The will also appoints an executor, or personal representative, to do the administrative work of finding and retitling assets, as well as finding all the beneficiaries. If minor or incapacitated children are involved, the will can also appoint a guardian to protect their interests.

  The administration of a will is typically done through the probate court process, the judicial process of administering an estate. Probate can be expensive and time-consuming, and everything becomes a matter of public record. Usually, probate is thought of negatively because of the time and expense involved. However, probate can be helpful when it comes to creditors. When the court is involved, creditors have a shortened period of time, known as the Creditor Claims Period, to come forward. If no probate estate is opened, creditors have a longer time period to file a claim against the estate or trust of the decedent. (Check your state laws regarding creditor claims period for a probate estate and, if no probate estate is opened, how long a creditor may have to file a claim against the estate.)

When a trust is in place (see below), a pour-over will is used. Basically, this type of will states that any asset not already transferred to the trust would "pour over" to the trust upon death. Pour-over wills do not act automatically because if the value of assets in the decedent's personal name exceed the state threshold for probate, a probate estate is required for those assets. Only when the probate estate is closed can the assets pour over into the trust.

- **By Trust.** A trust is a legal entity holding certain assets "in trust" on behalf of named beneficiaries. The grantor or settlor is the person who grants, settles and creates the trust. The trustee manages the assets on behalf of the beneficiaries, whom the assets are held to benefit.

  Trusts can help you maintain privacy and offer tremendous asset protection. They can also be used to help support disabled beneficiaries without losing public benefits.

  A trust is often thought of as a pre-arranged will. That's because it efficiently distributes assets without requiring them to pass through probate. As noted above, when a revocable living trust is in place, it is used in conjunction with a pour-over will.

  There are two basic types of trusts: **revocable trusts** and **irrevocable trusts.** It is revocable if you have the ability to amend, revoke or change the trust during your lifetime.

Since you maintain some control of the assets, they remain part of your taxable estate. For the most common type of trust, a revocable living trust, you are the grantor, trustee and beneficiary during your lifetime. It is only upon your death that someone else would act as trustee and take your place as beneficiary. Because you continue to have unfettered access and unfettered control over the revocable living trust, there is no asset protection during your lifetime. However, the revocable trust becomes irrevocable upon your death. That's done because, after you are gone, you do not want someone else to be able to change the terms of your documents. At that point, the assets you leave for others (a surviving spouse or children) can be asset-protected from the beneficiary's creditors. When properly drafted, the assets are held for their benefit and a creditor of a beneficiary cannot reach the assets.

A handful of states allow for self-settled irrevocable trusts — trusts where you create the trust for your own benefit for asset protection. But many other states have found it to be against public policy to create an irrevocable trust for your own benefit.

Generally, revocable trusts are used as the foundation of your estate plan and irrevocable trusts are used for more advanced estate planning. Irrevocable trusts are often used as gifting vehicles, meaning that you no longer control or own the assets. The assets in an irrevocable trust are typically moved out of your taxable gross estate and are no longer subject to estate taxes.

- **By Beneficiary Designation.** Every insurance policy provides the owner with an option to name beneficiaries who will receive the payment. You also filled out beneficiary designations when you opened an Individual Retirement

Account (IRA), 401(k), pension or annuity. Regardless of what your estate plan says, the beneficiary designations govern, so it is imperative that you confirm the beneficiary designation on assets comport with your estate plan.

- **By Operation of Law.** If you own property in partnership with another person, the contract may designate what happens to the property if one partner passes. Joint ownership of bank and brokerage accounts also dictates what happens to the ownership structure when one partner dies. Joint ownership can lead to unintended consequences as we will see in Chapter 2.

- **Intestate Succession.** If you die without an estate plan in place and have assets that are not addressed through beneficiary designation or joint ownership, your state provides a pecking order on how the estate will be distributed, which is known as the laws of intestate succession. Each state has its own nuances but, in many states, if the decedent is married with children, half will pass to the surviving spouse and half will pass to the children. If someone is single with children, the assets pass to the children in equal shares and, if someone is single without children, the assets pass to parents then siblings, etc. However, each state has its own pecking order. Regardless of the pecking order, if funds pass through intestate succession to a minor child, a guardian estate must be opened for each minor child and the guardian must report annually to the court on how the funds are used.

To see how dangerous this can be, consider the case of an Illinois man who died without an estate plan. Certainly, he intended to provide for his wife, but under the state's intestate succession rules, half his estate went to his wife and half to his children. Unfortunately, 50% of the estate was not enough to take care of his wife who was too old to re-enter the workforce. She ended up in the embarrassing position of asking the children to consider helping her out financially.

At least his children were adults. Consider the additional complexity of passing money to minor children without an estate plan. In these cases, monies must be routed through a guardian of the estate who is charged with handling the property and financial affairs of minor children.

The Four Basic Tools of Estate Planning

Your estate plan should seek to minimize taxes, avoid the courts, protect assets and leave a legacy. Building an effective estate plan to accomplish these goals is like building a house. You start with a solid foundation and add layers to meet specific needs. There are four basic tools we almost always use.

Your estate plan should seek to minimize taxes, avoid the courts, protect assets and leave a legacy

---

1. **Revocable Living Trusts**
   Because they are the most efficient tool for tax planning, avoiding probate and layering in asset protection for beneficiaries, a revocable living trust is the foundation for any solid estate plan. A well-executed and fully funded revocable living trust works to keep your estate out of probate since they detail how to hold, administer and distribute your assets for your beneficiaries upon your death.

   With a revocable trust, you can maintain control of your

assets during your lifetime, even moving them in and out as you desire. Upon your death, the revocable trust becomes irrevocable. This is a critical distinction if the trust is to live on for a period of time in order to provide asset protection, estate tax planning benefits or care for a minor or someone with special needs.

2. Pour-Over Will

A basic will details your wishes but would typically require a probate estate to be opened in order to do so. If you have a revocable living trust as the foundation of your plan, the hope is that a will is never used. But just in case, a pour-over will provides that any assets that were not transferred to your revocable living trust would pour-over into your trust upon death. It is important to note that the pour-over provision is not automatic. Rather, if the value of assets in your estate exceeds the threshold, a probate estate is opened and the assets held in your individual name pour into the trust only when the estate is closed.

3. Power of Attorney for Property

When you have a revocable living trust as part of your plan and have properly funded the trust (moved assets into the trust), the successor trustee comes into power when you die or become incapacitated.

But what happens to assets you forgot to move into your trust or purposefully left out — like a checking account with a nominal amount in it or retirement plan assets that cannot be moved into your revocable living trust? The power of attorney for property acts as a catch-all and appoints an agent to manage assets in your individual name. Most states allow for the agent to have a springing power, whereby they can only act in the event of your incapacity. However, some states, like Florida, require the agent to have the power to act immediately. The agent is always held to a fiduciary duty and must make financial decisions that are in your best interests and cannot use any of your money for their personal or corporate needs.

4. Power of Attorney for Healthcare

This document appoints a trusted relative or friend to make medical decisions for you in the event you are unable to make them for yourself.

A power of attorney for healthcare is different than a living will which makes your end-of-life desires known to healthcare providers in case you lose the ability to state them yourself. Today, many states have statutory forms for the power of attorney for healthcare that incorporate the option to indicate whether quality of life is important to you, which means that a living will is not always necessary.

The art of estate planning lies in how these tools can be wielded to create the perfect plan for your specific needs. One where the assets you've built up through a lifetime of work can transfer with minimal or no taxes, outside of the court process, and to the people and organizations you choose.

Basic Wills vs. Pour-Over Wills

A basic will is a map for probate to follow. If an estate, or parts of an estate, is to be distributed without benefit of a trust, a basic will provides instructions to the courts concerning how and to whom assets are to be dispersed. An executor is appointed either by the will or the court to collect all assets, pay creditors and distribute the balance in accordance with the will's instructions.

Although a will makes your desires known, it can be challenged or even interpreted differently than you intended. If, for some reason, you chose to exclude a child fighting addiction issues from your will, it would be in their best interest to contest the will.

Basic wills do not allow you to avoid the court process, which is expensive and time consuming, and everything becomes a matter of public record. Just as concerning is the time it takes the court to administer a will; putting assets into limbo while heirs wait for your bequest. It is possible for a basic will to include a "testamentary trust" which is created upon death. However, by the time a will incorporates proper trust provisions, it would be more efficient to have a revocable living trust to ensure the assets avoid probate.

For this reason, an estate planning attorney typically recommends that people have a revocable living trust and use a pour-over will to "pour over" any remaining assets into the revocable living trust. However, like a basic will, a pour-over will must pass through probate meaning distribution will be delayed. Therefore, the goal is to move virtually all of your assets into your revocable living trust so that probate can be avoided and hopefully the pour-over will never needs to be used.

The Most Common Mistakes People Make Setting Up Estate Plans

Sometimes things get overlooked. This happens with wills as easily as other things in life. Setting up a good, enforceable will doesn't have to be difficult, but missing some details can have a profound effect and require probate.

Setting up a good, enforceable will doesn't have to be difficult

Don't forget. The most basic mistake is simply forgetting about certain assets. Perhaps you knew your youngest daughter really wanted her grandmother's china but you forget to document it in your will. It becomes the executor or trustee's call rather than yours.

Pick good people. Speaking of executors and trustees, be sure you've selected the right person. Your oldest child may be a dreamer who doesn't like conflict or details. Before he knows it, the work of executing your estate plan gets out of hand causing needless family conflict and a delay in distributing your assets.

Beware of future financial traps. If you own a business or substantial illiquid assets, you could potentially saddle your heirs with hefty financial burdens. Depending on the size of your estate, there could be expensive estate or income taxes due and few liquid assets to sell off to pay the liabilities. In cases like this, your children may be forced to borrow substantial sums of money just to maintain ownership of assets you wanted them to have — or force the family to sell the business in order to have the necessary funds to pay the estate taxes.

Similar problems may plague a business when participating siblings are forced to buy out those not involved in the business. It is easy to see how debt could easily create problems with the business you took a lifetime to create.

Take care of the kids. Finally, there are too many instances where people have died unexpectedly without naming a guardian for minor children. When creating your will, you have the opportunity to appoint legal and financial guardians to act in your place. If you don't name the guardians, the courts will, and you probably don't want the judge to make such intimate decisions about your children's future.

Don't try this at home. For many people who attempt to draft their own wills, there are conflicting provisions or missing information which can result in litigation among the beneficiaries. In addition, most of the wills people draft on their own are not executed with the proper formalities so would likely be deemed invalid.

Lessons from the First Lady of Soul

Like millions around the world, I loved Aretha Franklin. Not just her music, but her "I am woman" style, love of her community and her many religious and secular passions.

I was so surprised how this magnificent humanitarian died without a will or trust. I remember hearing that some people thought it would be a great idea to donate Aretha's beautiful fur coats to either PETA for fundraising efforts or the homeless to help them stay warm through cold Detroit winters. Both are admirable desires, but nowhere is there a hint these were Aretha Franklin's desires. A woman with her immense intellect and creativity probably could have come up with some ideas in line with her own passions. With her cancer diagnosis it is surprising estate planning did not become a priority.

Her sizable financial estate faced a similar scenario. Given the state laws governing intestate succession (when someone dies without an estate plan in place), a single woman's children can expect to inherit the estate equally. However, this much money means "shirttail relatives" can be counted on to quickly appear. These distant relatives tend to stall distribution of the estate and practically guarantee much of the estate will disappear to pay substantial legal bills.

A little bit of time with an estate planning attorney could have helped Ms. Franklin avoid the mess. They would most likely have set up a revocable living trust that named beneficiaries and established the legacy she chose to leave behind. Why she didn't do this is a mystery to everyone involved.

Now, "Think!" about how different things would have been if Aretha Franklin had a pour-over will and a revocable living trust. The pour-over will would have detailed that all property she owned at death and not specifically left to someone was to be put into her revocable living trust. All would have been well and good as the only named beneficiaries of her trust, her four children, would inherit all the assets.

An estate like Aretha Franklin's probably had a number of complex twists and turns. With her wide-ranging passions, there were probably any number of organizations she may have wanted to support, and I doubt she wanted her personal financial information and family drama open to public view. There may well have been creditors who had, or supposed they had, claims on many of her assets, and that information would become public information while moving through probate.

If Aretha properly retitled assets from her name to her revocable living trust, the assets subject to the pour-over will would be small and probate could be avoided. Her estate and trust could have been administered privately, decision-making would have been streamlined, and the assets left to her family could have been asset protected from their creditors and could have allowed for the maximum amount to pass estate tax free from generation to generation. This concept of generation skipping transfer tax planning (or GST planning) is discussed further in Chapters 2 and 9. Knowing that her estate would be subject to hundreds of millions of dollars in estate tax liabilities, she could have devised a more meaningful way to leave a legacy. Given her passion for her church and community, she could have left some of the song rights to a foundation or charity, avoiding estate taxes on what was left and transforming her community. The moral of the story is to develop a good estate plan…keep it up to date and have some R-E-S-P-E-C-T to determine the legacy you wish to leave.

Every life has complications. An effective plan straightens things out before you die and before all manner of confusion breaks loose.

Chapter 2
Estate Taxes

What Constitutes Your Gross Estate?

First, let's consider what assets could be subject to taxes when someone dies. Your "taxable gross estate" is a legal term, and it includes everything the decedent (person who died) has accumulated during their life and anything the decedent had ownership or control over. Unless you engage in advanced estate planning, it all becomes fair game for taxation.

Most people own property, including real estate and tangible personal property. Real estate includes your home, rental properties, vacation homes and any other real estate you may have accumulated over your lifetime. Then there's all the personal property you can touch and feel — fur coats, art, cars, boats, dishes, furniture, keepsakes, tools, family heirlooms and more. Most people are astonished at how much they really own and rarely do people keep an updated list of these tangible assets. Yet, personal belongings can cause some of the biggest fights if someone dies without documenting how, and to whom, they want their personal property distributed.

You also probably own intangible property, things you can't touch and feel, but have value — checking accounts, savings accounts, IRAs, pensions and other retirement plans, partnerships, stocks, bonds and investments. All of these assets are part of your gross estate. And in today's internet age, digital assets are also considered.

One asset often overlooked is life insurance, often touted as a tax-free investment. The death benefit on life insurance policies are always income tax free, meaning the beneficiary does not have to pay income tax on the death benefit. However, if the policy was owned by you at the time of your death, the death benefit of the policy is included in your taxable gross estate. Even a term life insurance policy with $0 cash value and a death benefit of $2 million would add an additional $2 million to your taxable gross estate. Many people purchase large life insurance policies...so large they push the value of their estate over the tax exemption threshold. Without proper planning, the valuable gift you planned to leave your family can automatically become a lot less valuable.

WHAT CONSTITUTES A GROSS ESTATE
Examples of tangible & intangible assets

Tangible
(Can be touched)

- Real Estate
- Vehicles
- Household Items
- Art
- Family Heirlooms
- Pets & Animals
- Jewelry
- Clothing
- Collectibles

Intangible
(No physical presence)

- IRAs/Pensions
- Investments
- Businesses
- Digital Assets
- Intellectual Property
- Trademarks
- Life Insurance Death Benefits

What Taxes Will You Owe?

Before discussing how to minimize your taxes, let's look at the taxes your estate, or those who inherit your estate, could owe upon your death.

- **Federal Estate Taxes.** These are levied on the total assets you own above the federal exemption level. As of 2022, those amounts are $12.06 million per person or $24.12 million per couple, adjusted for inflation annually. However, under current tax law, this exemption reverts to only $5 million, inflation adjusted, in 2026, which is an important point to remember. Because the tax laws and your net worth are always changing, it is important to know where your taxable gross estate is relative to the exemption levels.

- **State Estate Taxes.** Gross assets above the state exemption level, which differs from state to state, are taxable. When the state exemption is lower than the federal exemption, only state taxes are levied on the amount up to the federal exemption. Above that level, state and federal taxes are combined. (See Chapter 16 for state thresholds.)

  However, if you live in New York, the state level estate tax can be especially confusing. Under the systems used by other states (and the federal government), if an estate is large enough to be subject to the tax, only the amount over the exemption level is taxed. By contrast, New York taxes the entire value of any estate that exceeds the exemption level. This can lead to some interesting situations discussed further in Chapter 3.

- **Income Taxes.** Under current tax laws, assets included in your taxable gross estate get a step-up in basis to fair market value at the time of death. However, advanced estate planning tools often look to move assets outside of your taxable gross estate. If an asset is outside of your taxable gross estate at death, you do not get a step-up in basis. Here's how that would play out.

Let's assume you owned an asset that was originally purchased for $100,000 and is worth $500,000 at the time of your death. In this case, your estate (or trust) would include this asset in your taxable gross estate and it would get a step-up in basis to fair market value of $500,000. When your heirs turn around and sell the asset, no capital gains tax is owed.

In contrast, if you gifted the $100,000 asset during your lifetime and the asset was worth $500,000 at the time of death, it would all pass outside of your taxable gross estate. In this instance, you gifted the current value and future appreciation. But if you gifted the asset before your death so that it was not included in your estate, the person who received the gift would take your cost basis in the asset of $100,000. If they sold the asset after your death, they would have to pay capital gains tax on the appreciation. In these cases, there is a delicate balance between estate tax and income tax planning, which will be explored further in Chapter 3.

- **Gift Taxes.** During your lifetime, you may make gifts up to the annual gift exemption for "free." As of 2022, the amount is $16,000 per person (or $32,000 for a married couple). No taxes are levied on annual exclusion gifts.

In addition to annual exclusion gifts, you have a lifetime gift exemption equal to the federal estate exemption. Thus, as of 2022, you can gift $12.06 million upon your death — or during your lifetime. All gifts made during your lifetime over the annual exclusion amount will be deducted from the amount you can pass estate tax free at death, and you'll need to file a gift tax return with the IRS. No gift tax is owed if you are within the lifetime exemptions, but you must inform the IRS that you have used up a portion of your lifetime gift exemption. For example, considering the current tax laws, if you gift $8 million to your children during your lifetime while the exemption is $12.06 million, your remaining estate exemption at death will only be $4.06 million.

When Congress passed the Tax Cuts and Jobs Act, lawmakers realized that potential problems will occur when the exemption and lifetime gifting amounts revert in 2026. The challenge is that in order to calculate an estate tax liability, the IRS requires for all lifetime gifts to be added back into the taxable gross estate at death.

Imagine a person gifted the full $11 million of her lifetime exemption and dies in 2026 when the exemption is only $5 million. This initially created cause for concern because any lifetime gifts are included in the taxable gross estate for purposes of calculating the estate-tax liability. If a person gifted $11 million of lifetime exemption this year and dies in 2026 with only $3 million, the value of the person's taxable gross estate would be $14 million with an exemption of only $5 million. Therefore, the estate would owe federal estate tax at a rate of 40% on every dollar over $5 million (40% of $9 million = $3.6 million), which is in excess of the $3 million in the estate.

In 2018, the Treasury released proposed regulations which helped mitigate concerns of clawback, and in November 2019 the final regulations were issued. Specifically, there would not be an estate tax on assets gifted when the exclusion covered the gift. The estate would only pay tax on the $3 million in assets. These final taxpayer-friendly regulations have sent advisory teams for high-net-worth people scurrying to use their entire lifetime exemption ($12.06 million in 2022) before they lose it!

- **Inheritance Taxes.** These are the taxes paid by those who inherit your assets. While most states tax at the estate level, some states tax at the beneficiary level. (See Chapter 16 for states which tax beneficiaries on their inheritance.)

The Difference between Estate and Inheritance Taxes

Today, six states have inheritance taxes. The difference lies in who pays the tax. Estate taxes are levied on the right to pass assets on. Inheritance taxes are levied on the right to receive assets from an estate. In other words, an estate pays estate taxes while an inheritor pays inheritance taxes. (See Chapter 16 for state estate tax thresholds and which states have inheritance taxes.)

An estate pays estate taxes while an inheritor pays inheritance taxes

There are exceptions, and they always depend on how close a relative is to you. Assets can always be transferred to a surviving spouse without any inheritance taxes being levied. Children and grandchildren are exempt from inheritance taxes in some states. Further removed relatives such as sisters, brothers, nieces and nephews usually pay some inheritance tax. And inheritors who are not at all related always pay (unless the inheritor is a charity). Some wills direct that an estate pay the inheritance tax for the beneficiaries.

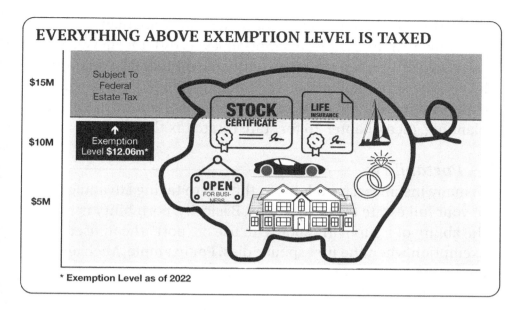

EVERYTHING ABOVE EXEMPTION LEVEL IS TAXED

* Exemption Level as of 2022

— *Estate tax exemptions* —

Federal estate and inheritance taxes get all the media attention, but 99.9% of the people who die in America do so without paying federal estate taxes. Based on the year in which you die, the government allows you to pass a certain amount of money estate tax free. Under the Tax Cuts and Jobs Act of 2017 (TCJA), the estate tax exemption was doubled to $10 million adjusted for inflation through the end of 2025. Once again, in 2026 the exemption is scheduled to drop to $5 million adjusted for inflation. With the 2022 exemption set at $12.06 million for one person, only 0.1% of all estates even need to worry about federal estate taxes.

However, for those who do pass away owning assets in excess of the exemption, the federal government levies an estate tax at a rate of 40% on every dollar over the exemption. If you have a sizable estate, putting off your estate planning until it is too late can cost you a small fortune.

State estate tax, income and inheritance taxes are likely to affect many more people. Exemption levels differ from state to state, and only seven states currently mirror federal exemption levels. The state exemptions vary dramatically, so where you expect to live when you die can play an important role in estate planning. (See Chapter 16 for state estate tax thresholds.)

— *Portability* —

In many instances, portability is the key to taking advantage of your full estate tax exemptions. Basically, portability is the ability of a surviving spouse to use or "port" the unused exemption when the first spouse dies. For example, Michael dies in 2022 with a $3 million estate. He was allowed to leave $12.06 million estate tax free, so $9.06 million of his person exemption was unused. This amount is available to "port" to Marcia's estate, meaning she now has the exemption available at the time of her death plus an additional $9.06 million worth of estate and gift exemptions available to her.

This could really come in handy if Congress chooses not to renew the expanded exemptions from the TCJA and the individual exemption reverts to $5 million adjusted for inflation. Armed with portability, even in 2026, Marcia will still have at least $14.06 million worth of exemptions available.

However, portability is not automatic. It must be part of a thoughtful plan of action. In order to capture portability, the executor, trustee or personal representative of Michael's estate must file an estate tax return. Although no estate tax is owed, it is necessary to file in order to make a "portability election" to transfer, or "port," any part of the estate tax not used for Michael's estate to Marcia's estate. Hopefully Marcia will live many more years and her estate will enjoy a large exemption when she passes.

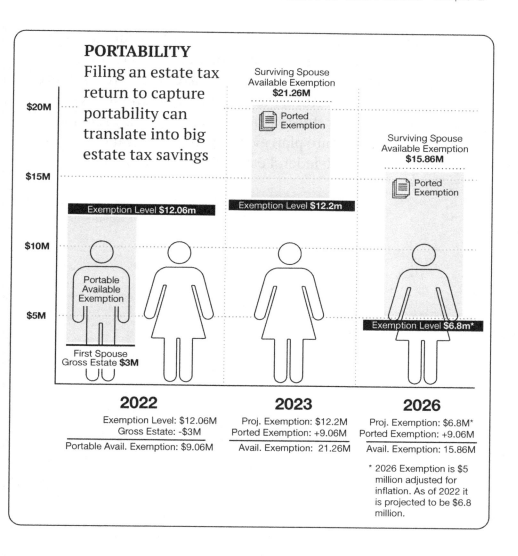

PORTABILITY

Filing an estate tax return to capture portability can translate into big estate tax savings

Surviving Spouse Available Exemption **$21.26M**

Ported Exemption

Surviving Spouse Available Exemption **$15.86M**

Ported Exemption

$20M

$15M

$10M

$5M

Exemption Level **$12.06m**

Exemption Level **$12.2m**

Portable Available Exemption

Exemption Level **$6.8m***

First Spouse Gross Estate **$3M**

2022
Exemption Level: $12.06M
Gross Estate: -$3M
_____
Portable Avail. Exemption: $9.06M

2023
Proj. Exemption: $12.2M
Ported Exemption: +9.06M
_____
Avail. Exemption: 21.26M

2026
Proj. Exemption: $6.8M*
Ported Exemption: +9.06M
_____
Avail. Exemption: 15.86M

* 2026 Exemption is $5 million adjusted for inflation. As of 2022 it is projected to be $6.8 million.

Since you never know who will die first, how much will end up in their estates or what the tax laws will be, married couples are often encouraged to have roughly equal values in their estates. This can be done by transferring assets between spouses. This is considered gifting, and there is no limitation on the gifts married couples can make to one another.

Portability helps you take advantage of your full exemption

at the federal level. However, many states with estate tax exemptions do not recognize portability at the state level. Although portability can help mitigate taxes at the federal level, you may lose the opportunity to pass money without paying state estate taxes. For this reason, tax planning may remain important to your estate plan even if your gross taxable estate does not approach the federal estate tax exemption level.

Chapter 3
The Four Basic Principles of Estate Planning

Most people's eyes glaze over when they begin to read about something as complex as estate planning because of the myriad federal and state laws that affect each decision. However, at the heart of this convoluted estate planning process are four simple principles on which everything rests:

- Minimize taxes
- Avoid court
- Protect assets
- Leave the desired legacy

Every one of these principles could, themselves, be the subject of an entire book. The way they work together to create a good estate plan is the artistry of the estate planning attorney.

PRINCIPLE ONE: Minimize Taxes

A significant part of most people's lives is spent chasing financial success. As your estate reaches the tax exemption thresholds, it could be subject to taxes as high as 50%. Therefore, you need to be proactive in your planning to minimize and, in some instances, completely avoid egregious estate taxes.

Because you only have to pay taxes on what you own (or control) at the time of your death, you need to minimize the value of assets in your name without just giving it all away without a plan. Since it is virtually impossible to plan your exit from the world with such precision that you "leave your last dollar to the undertaker," estate planning tools such as trusts and gifts play an important role, allowing you to move hard-earned assets out of your taxable gross estate.

As noted above, the estate tax and income tax planning nuances are dizzying and complex, but it is such a material element, I feel the need to delve into detail. **If the thought of such a tax discussion makes your skin crawl, feel free to skip to Page 62 to learn how a proper plan helps you to avoid the courts and layers in asset protection for beneficiaries.**

You only have to pay taxes on what you own (or control) at the time of your death

— *Who owns what?*

When seeking to minimize taxes, ownership matters. If you still maintain control of an asset, whether through ownership in your individual name or a revocable living trust, it is part of your taxable estate subject to estate tax exemptions. However, it you have "gifted" an asset, giving full ownership to another person or entity, it is no longer in your estate and, therefore, no longer part of your taxable gross estate.

Privacy needs are critical for many people. If you spent your life without broadcasting everything you own, you probably want to make sure your treasured secrets are not broadcast to the world when you die. A will is a public document. A trust is not.

— *Revocable living trusts*

Revocable living trusts can help to minimize potential taxes, avoid the court system and layer in asset protection for beneficiaries. Since assets in a revocable trust already have designated beneficiaries, they do not have to go through probate, allowing for speedier distribution of assets to beneficiaries after your death.

For married couples, a revocable living trust is a critical tax planning tool to ensure:
- No federal estate tax is owed until both spouses have passed away
- No state estate tax is owed until both spouses have passed away
- Each spouse can pass $12.06 million estate tax free to the next generation (or $24.12 million as a couple) based on 2022 exemption levels, which will change in 2026
- Where estate tax planning is not of concern, income tax planning is layered in to minimize as much as 23.8% in income taxes for the next generation

In addition, trusts provide the best mechanism to control the flow of fund — ensuring assets pass to children or other designated beneficiaries (instead of the pool boy).

Marital trusts are the foundation of estate planning for married couples. How they are used today is discussed in detail in the next chapter.

Planning for generation skipping transfer taxes (GST) should also be considered when setting up revocable living trusts for both married couples and single people. Basically, skip transfers were originally set up to avoid repeated payment of estate taxes as assets passed from parents to children to grandchildren and beyond. In an effort to recapture at least part of these taxes, the federal government limits the amount that can pass in a GST tax exempt transfer. Under the current law, GST is subject to the same exemption levels as estate and gift taxes, which will be $12.06 million in 2022.

Sometimes GST planning refers to skipping over one generation to the next — skipping over a child and leaving assets to a grandchild. Other times, GST planning refers to leaving assets to a child in a fashion, making the assets available for the child, but if the child does not need the funds, they can pass estate tax free to grandchildren. Imagine Susie inherits $3 million from her parents in a GST exempt trust. Successful in her own right, Susie does not need the money and the $3 million grows to $6 million during her lifetime. If the trust was properly structured to qualify as being GST exempt, upon Susie's death the entire $6 million can pass estate tax free to her children. Generation skipping is discussed more thoroughly in Chapter 9.

— *Irrevocable gift trusts*

This type of trust typically removes assets from your control and puts them in the hands of a trustee with designated beneficiaries whose interests become primary. Since you no longer own or exert control of the assets, irrevocable gift trusts remove the assets from your estate eliminating both probate and estate tax concerns.

Irrevocable gift trusts are key to minimizing estate taxes for anyone with an estate expected to exceed the state or federal estate tax exemption levels. Knowing that you want your children to inherit certain assets, it behooves you to engage in thoughtful gifting to strategically move assets outside of your taxable gross estate over time. In doing so, you transfer not only the current value of the gift but also all future appreciation outside of your estate. Remember, if you gift assets in excess of the annual exclusion amount, an informational gift tax return must be filed to notify the IRS that you have used up a portion of your lifetime exemption.

— *Minimizing taxes means more than just estate taxes* —

Traditionally, when the exemption (the amount you could pass estate tax free at death) was much lower, many more families were subject to estate taxes. Estate tax minimization was a larger concern because the estate tax rates of 40% at the federal level alone were higher than most income tax rates. As the federal estate tax exemption continued to grow, fewer individuals were faced with potential estate tax liabilities. As a result, many practitioners began to shift their focus from minimizing estate taxes to minimizing income taxes. Minimizing income taxes can potentially save the next generation 23.8% in capital gains taxes, including a 20% capital gains tax and 3.8% Medicare tax. At the end of the day, for a married couple, tax planning should always be at the forefront of discussions, but your attorney may suggest whether you should prioritize estate or income tax minimization based on your personal situation.

Tax law related to estate planning is, in many ways, like playing three-dimensional chess

— *The 3-D chess game of exemptions and income taxes* —

The complexity of tax law is a burden in its own right. However, tax law related to estate planning is, in many ways, like playing three-dimensional chess. Federal and state governments dictate different laws, exemptions and rates. In many locales, any degree of wealth is subject to estate taxes, inheritance taxes or both. Furthermore, tax laws may change at any time — as will your net worth or taxable gross estate.

Consider how this situation would play out in my home state of Illinois. Brigitte dies in 2022 with an estate worth $15 million. The estate would be subject to federal estate taxes of 40% on the amount in excess of the $12.06 million exemption. The $2.94 million left over the exemption level would also be subject to state estate taxes. When an estate is subject to both state and federal taxes, the state-level estate tax calculation is circular in nature, allowing credit at one level for paying taxes on another. This often translates into a marginal state-level tax of 10%. That means Brigitte's estate would be subject to a 50% tax on the $2.94 million above the federal exemption level. That's $1.47 million from Brigitte's estate in taxes.

And there's more. Since the exemption in Illinois is only $4 million, her estate is also subject to Illinois estate taxes on the amount from $4 million to $12.06 million. The Illinois estate tax rate is graduated up to 16% plus a base amount. In reality, when you run the numbers on the Illinois attorney general's estate tax calculator, the Illinois tax starts at a rate of 28.5% and tapers off to 10%. For Brigitte, the Illinois tax on the amount subject only to Illinois estate tax is in excess of $1 million.

Thus, the full tax burden on Brigitte's estate of federal and estate taxes is more than $2.65 million. Take my word for it; Illinois is a great place to live, but an expensive place to die in. There are better places to die for people of means, unless they engage in thoughtful planning to minimize or avoid estate tax consequences.

Illinois is not alone. Several other states across the country also levy hefty estate taxes. Remember that state thresholds vary dramatically as detailed on Chapter 16.

However, New York is the only state to levy state estate taxes on the value of the entire estate not just the portion exceeding the state or federal estate tax exemption level. This has led to some situations where the portion of the estate in excess of the New York estate tax exemption is taxed at rates exceeding 100%. This is referred to as the New York estate tax cliff.

Here's an example to show how this happens. In 2021, the New York estate tax exemption was $5.93 million. If an individual passed away in 2021 with a taxable estate of $5.93 million, no New York estate tax is due and the full $5.93 million will pass to his beneficiaries. However, if that same individual left a taxable estate just $70,000 higher, his estate would owe $171,840 in New York estate taxes, leaving only $5,828,160 for his beneficiaries. In other words, his beneficiaries would receive less from a $6 million estate than from a $5.93 million estate!

To mitigate this risk, trusts can include a provision for a conditional charitable bequest of estate assets in excess of the New York exemption amount. Imagine leaving the $70,000 excess to charity instead of causing a $170,000 estate tax liability. This provision will only apply if the excess that would go to charity is less than the New York estate tax that would be due if the gift to charity was not made. By being proactive with the planning and drafting, beneficiaries receive the maximum amount possible (in some instances even more) and the excess which triggers estate tax goes to charity — a win all the way around.

— *Step-up in basis is key to minimizing income taxes*
A number of years ago, Congress gave a break to families who diligently built wealth through long-term investing. It allowed the beneficiaries of these estates to inherit assets at fair market value on the day they transferred ownership, which means that the original purchase price became irrelevant. By taking

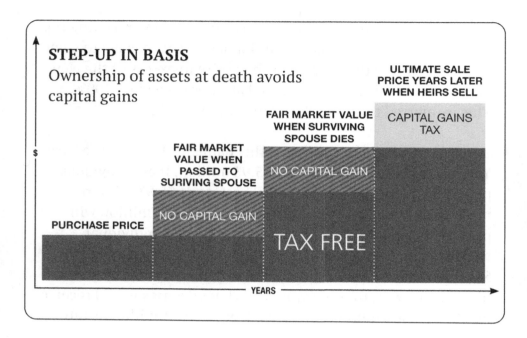

STEP-UP IN BASIS
Ownership of assets at death avoids capital gains

ULTIMATE SALE
PRICE YEARS LATER
WHEN HEIRS SELL

FAIR MARKET VALUE
WHEN SURVIVING
SPOUSE DIES

CAPITAL GAINS
TAX

FAIR MARKET
VALUE WHEN
PASSED TO
SURIVING SPOUSE

NO CAPITAL GAIN

PURCHASE PRICE

NO CAPITAL GAIN

TAX FREE

$

YEARS

a step-up in basis, when the family turns around and sells the inherited assets, they are able to avoid income tax on any appreciation.

A parent may have purchased shares of stock in Intel for $3,500 back in 1978. After holding the stock for more than four decades, it is now worth $2,517,058; a great buy all around. If the children were forced to pay capital gains on this good investment, it would lower the value of the stock by over a half million dollars to $2,013,646 (multiply the $2,513,558 in accumulated value by the .238 federal capital gains plus Medicare taxes). Instead, Congress allowed the beneficiaries to take a "step-up in basis" to the fair market value on the day of death. Therefore, if the asset was sold shortly after death, the family would not have to pay any income tax on the appreciation of the asset.

With a properly structured trust, the value of the asset steps up a second time when the second spouse dies. In other words, no income tax would be owed and the children would inherit the full value of what their parents built up over a lifetime. However, if the estate exceeds state or federal estate tax exemption levels, those taxes would still be due.

You also have to account for the fact you likely don't know when you or your spouse will die. If someone died during the economic recession of 2008, the assets in their estate likely had a step-down in basis creating an even bigger income tax liability if the surviving spouse died during a market upturn. The key to minimizing potential capital gains taxes is getting a step-up in basis — akin to a market rate adjustment — at the time property passes to the beneficiaries.

If you are married, be sure to read Chapter 4 to see in more detail the ways an estate plan can teeter-totter between working to minimize estate taxes or income taxes.

— *Trusts in community property vs. common law states*

Revocable living trusts are relatively easy to set up; however, there are also state considerations to take into account, especially related to the difference between community property and common law (non-community property) states.

Ownership issues are key. In community property states (currently nine states), couples are viewed as a single unit owning all assets acquired during a marriage. Alaska, Florida, Tennessee and South Dakota allow residents to "opt in" to community property through trust planning. (See Chapter 16 for Community Property vs. Common Law Property States.)

In common law states, couples are viewed as two individuals.

The distinction requires a different structural approach to the design of their revocable living trusts.

Consider what happens to two different couples, both named Harry and Sally. Harry and Sally Anderson live in a community property state, while Harry and Sally Burton live in a common law state. Both couples paid $300,000 for an investment that increased in market value to $1 million by the time they died, and both couples own their investments together. Tax law allows a step-up in basis valuation when the first spouse dies. Here's where things head down different paths.

Harry and Sally Anderson live in a community property state... The investment and almost all the other assets they own are considered to be owned by them as a single unit. When Harry Anderson dies, community property law allows for a step-up in tax basis on the entire investment, $1 million. Thus, when it passed to a beneficiary or sold for $1 million, no income tax would have to be paid.

Harry and Sally Burton live in a common law state... Since ownership in the investment is divided between two units, only Harry's half of the investment receives a step-up in tax basis. Sally's half does not. The tax basis for her half of the purchase price was $150,000 and the sale price for her half of the sale was $500,000. She has to pay capital gains (20%) plus Medicare tax (3.8%) on $350,000 or $83,300.

For this reason, the structure of a revocable living trust for a married couple who reside in a community property state is often a single trust, whereas the structure of a revocable living trust for a married couple who resides in a non-community property state is often two separate trusts which are virtually identical. Either way, assets can be owned by both parties (or both trusts).

RESIDENCY IMPACT OF STEP-UP IN BASIS
At death of second spouse

The Andersons
Reside in Community Property state

Current Value: $1 Million
Purchase Price: $300,000
Capital Gain: $700,000

Step Up when Harry Dies: $1 Million
Sally Owes Taxes on: $0
Income Taxes Due: $0

The Burtons
Reside in Common Law state

Current Value: $1 Million
Purchase Price: $300,000 ($150,000 ea.)
Capital Gain: $300,000 ($150,000 ea.)

Income
Taxes Due:
$83,300

Step Up on Harry's Half: $500,000
Sally Owes Taxes on: $350,000
Income Taxes Due When Sally Dies: $83,300

It is easy to see how the ability to step-up an asset's value when the second spouse dies, without paying capital gains tax, could significantly increase bottom line value by minimizing, or even eliminating, the amount of capital gains to be paid.

Many couples turn to joint titling in an attempt to equally divide assets, especially couples living in common law states. However, this is really a Band-Aid solution preventing them from taking advantage of estate planning tools designed to minimize taxes and protect assets.

It is important to compare joint titling to more sophisticated estate planning tools.

— *Two trusts are better than one and any trust is better than joint titling*

Joint titling and joint trusts are attractive options for many people, especially when entering their first marriage. At the beginning of a marriage, many couples feel it is important to "share and share alike" rather than focus on their future estate planning needs. For couples who live in a community property state, a properly drafted community property joint trust can provide the necessary mechanisms for asset protection and income tax minimization. However, if you reside in a state that is NOT community property, a "joint trust" can have many dangers.

Asset protection. First, understand that joint titling means you both own something equally as joint tenants. One can't sell one part of the asset, take their money and go home. Either you both sell or no one sells and, if one of you is sued, the entire asset is at risk.

Joint ownership does not provide any asset protection for the surviving spouse. Upon the first spouse's death, everything passes to the surviving spouse and is reachable by the surviving spouse's creditors. However, if assets are passed through a revocable living trust, the surviving spouse could be entitled to asset protection.

Minimizing taxes. Joint titling presents possible estate tax complications. If assets are jointly titled, they are held in your names rather than a trust and could create estate tax liabilities. Imagine Harry and Sally relied on joint ownership for all assets. When Harry died, all assets would pass to the Sally outright by operation of law. When Sally subsequently died, she would have the ability to pass the exemption amount tax free to the children. Thus, by relying on joint ownership as a Band-Aid solution, Harry and Sally can only pass $12.06 million tax free at the federal level — or $4 million as Illinois residents — instead of double the amount of the tax-free transfer by engaging in proper estate planning. On Sally's death, Harry could file an estate tax return to capture her unused exemption at the federal level, but Illinois does not recognize portability and they would have lost the ability to pass $4 million estate tax free at the state level.

Beneficiary designations. Separate trusts are often recommended when dealing with blended families. In each case, the use of separate trusts enables spouses to maintain control of who inherits their assets and allows for maximum estate tax planning so that each spouse can leverage their respective exemption. Separate trusts prevent the family of one spouse from losing their inheritance when the surviving spouse remarries or enters into another relationship.

— *Finding the right balance between estate and income tax concerns*

Federal estate taxes affect few estates, but state estate taxes affect many more, and income taxes affect every estate. Thus, finding the best estate plan solution is a delicate balance. Think of it as a teeter-totter. What is done on one side to minimize estate taxes may raise income tax liabilities. Finding the right balance depends on how trusts are structured to best meet an individual's personal and family needs. We will discuss setting up marital trusts in Chapter 4, where we take a more in-depth look at issues married couples need to discuss. However, recognize that when the tax laws changed to dramatically increase the amount you could pass estate tax free, much of the conversation moved away from federal estate tax planning to finding ways to minimize income taxes.

With the shift in focus to income tax planning, you'll want the structure to ensure that assets left to the surviving spouse are included in the surviving spouse's estate. Three ways to do this include:

- Outright distribution
- General power of appointment
- Qualified terminable interest property (QTIP) trust

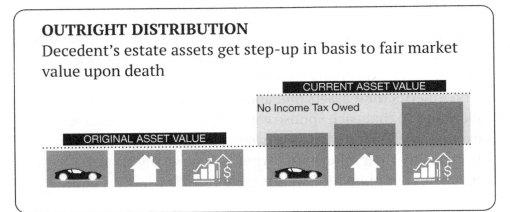

OUTRIGHT DISTRIBUTION
Decedent's estate assets get step-up in basis to fair market value upon death

CURRENT ASSET VALUE

No Income Tax Owed

ORIGINAL ASSET VALUE

The simplicity of outright distribution. There are, of course, other ways assets can be distributed to the surviving spouse upon the first spouse's death. Outright distribution is a neat and simple solution where the basis value of the assets are stepped-up on the first spouse's death and then receive a second step-up in basis on the surviving spouse's death. The risks here are that the surviving spouse may elect to leave the assets inherited to a new family and the assets inherited are reachable by the surviving spouse's creditors.

General power of appointment. An easy way to structure this would be to give the surviving spouse a general power of appointment over assets. A general power of appointment would enable the surviving spouse to designate where the balance of the assets would pass — to virtually anyone. By doing so, the IRS determines that the surviving spouse had so much control over the inheritance that the asset is included in the surviving spouse's taxable gross estate. This allows for a step-up in basis value on the first spouse's death and the surviving spouse's death, eliminating income tax on those assets. While this is an easy fix, the surviving spouse can elect to leave the balance of the trust inherited to anyone they wish, potentially leaving funds to the pool boy instead of children. If the funds are left in a trust where the spouse has a general power of appointment, no estate tax return is necessary.

Outright distribution and general power of appointment are also dangerous choices if the surviving spouse is elderly, frail or easily influenced. You lose control since assets become part of the surviving spouse's estate and may not be distributed as you intended. What happens if they remarry and the bulk of the money you worked to build up ends up with a new family rather than your own? Your estate would also not be the first to end up in the hands of a handsome pool boy or disreputable con artist.

Qualified terminable interest property (QTIP) trusts. QTIPs are a type of irrevocable trust commonly used to leverage tax planning. They allow people to take care of a loved one while maintaining control of how the trust's assets are distributed once the surviving spouse dies. In a nutshell, all income from the QTIP trust must be distributed to the surviving spouse, but you may elect to have principal distributed at the trustee's discretion, or none at all if it is believed that the surviving spouse has sufficient assets. When the surviving spouse dies, the principal and any leftover interest is distributed to the designated beneficiaries (or held in trust for their benefit). In many cases the designated beneficiaries are the decedent's children from a previous relationship. As marital trusts evolve, these type trusts are also often used to help minimize state estate taxes. This is discussed further in Chapter 4 where we talk about the recent evolution in marital trusts.

— *Trusts as an instrument of care* —

Revocable trusts are also valuable tools in managing your assets and care if you become mentally or physically incapacitated. They are equally valuable in caring for heirs who are unable to manage their affairs due to incapacitation, incompetence or spendthrift habits. In these cases, you select a trustee to manage the trust's assets and pay for the care of yourself or of designated beneficiaries.

In the case of a special needs child or other disabled person, a special needs trust could prove invaluable in making sure they are cared for throughout their entire life. These are irrevocable trusts solely for the purpose of paying for a disabled person's special needs. Money can be made available for their needs from many sources including life insurance policies or law suits, but the trust can be structured to ensure the assets are not considered countable for purposes of determining eligibility for federal or state support. In this way, the funds are available for the beneficiary's needs, but would not act to penalize the beneficiary for having generous relatives.

— *Beyond trusts: using gifts to reduce taxes* —

Since the key to reducing estate taxes is to reduce the amount of assets held in your name, gifting allows you to transfer wealth free of estate tax. Any asset can be gifted at any time to whomever you'd like. However, there are yearly and lifetime limits to the amount you can gift without paying gift taxes.

Unlimited annual gifting for married couples. Love is grand because married couples may make unlimited gifts to one another. I'm still enough of a romantic to believe a big part of gifting is love, but gifts certainly help leverage tax planning as

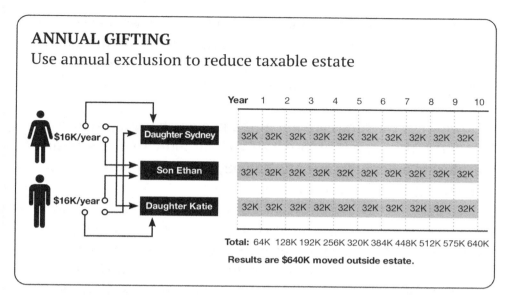

ANNUAL GIFTING
Use annual exclusion to reduce taxable estate

well. By moving assets from one spouse's name to the other's name — or from one revocable trust to the other's revocable trust — assets are simply moved from one balance sheet to the other. Where gifting really makes a difference in estate planning is when you can move assets off your balance sheets and outside of your taxable gross estates.

Annual gifting limits. As of 2022, you can gift up to $16,000 per year tax free to as many people as you'd like. A married couple can gift $32,000 tax free to each person. This annual amount is typically adjusted annually for inflation.

Annual gifting can be an incredible planning tool to minimize estate taxes. Imagine making gifts of $32,000 to someone every year over 10 years. That would effectively move $320,000 outside of your taxable gross estate. This translates into $128,000 of federal estate tax savings if you are above thresholds (40% tax on $320,000). However, the benefits are often even larger because we are not only moving the current value outside of your estate but also the appreciation. In other words, if the $320,000 in gifts grew to $500,000, we have moved even more. If this tool is used for multiple family members, the tax savings grow exponentially. And, the gift has no gift tax or income tax implications for the recipient.

However, if the funds are not gifted in a given year, you lose the opportunity — use it or lose it! If you gift more than the annual exclusion amount to any one person, you must report it to the IRS using a gift tax return.

Lifetime gifting limits. In addition to the annual gift limits, you are also able to make lifetime gifts. The current lifetime gift exemption is the same as the estate tax exemption. The Tax Cuts and Jobs Act (TCJA) lifted this exemption in 2019 from $5 million per person to $10 million per person, adjusted for inflation. In 2026 it is scheduled to drop back to $5 million per person, adjusted for inflation.

This exemption actually applies to the gift and estate tax combined. The IRS refers to this as a "unified credit." If you gift $2 million during your lifetime, this amount is deducted from the overall exemption level. If the estate tax exemption was $12.06 million, and you made lifetime gifts of $2 million, your exemption at death would be decreased to $10.06 million.

Any gifts in excess of the annual gift exclusion must be reported to the IRS on a gift tax return. Only in rare situations is gifting recommended when it creates a tax liability, like gifting in excess of the exemption. Thus, the gift tax returns are often for informational purposes only to notify the IRS that you have used up a portion of your lifetime exemption.

Once you gift an asset, it is typically off your balance sheet permanently unless you continue to retain ownership or

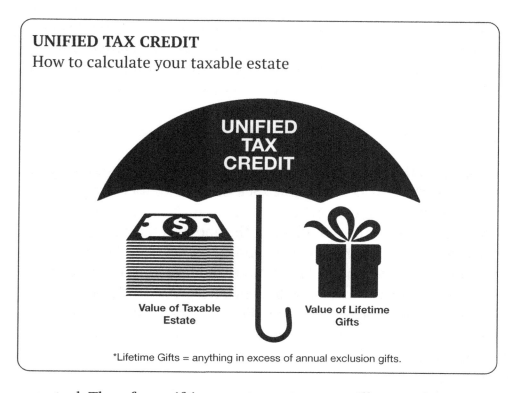

UNIFIED TAX CREDIT

How to calculate your taxable estate

UNIFIED
TAX
CREDIT

Value of Taxable
Estate

Value of Lifetime
Gifts

*Lifetime Gifts = anything in excess of annual exclusion gifts.

control. Therefore, gifting assets you expect will appreciate is a good idea. Imagine gifting a $1 million asset this year that is valued at $3 million at the time of your death. Through thoughtful planning, the asset and all of the related appreciation ($2 million in added value) is moved outside of your taxable gross estate. You've only used $1 million of your lifetime exemption and more of your estate remains available to your heirs.

Using direct pay to give money tax free. You can greatly expand annual and lifetime gifting limits by directly paying medical and educational expenses. Perhaps a favored nephew is studying for a graduate degree and you'd like to help out with tuition expenses. By directly paying the university, you can relieve his educational expenses without affecting any gift or estate limits. In fact, you could still give him the annual gift exclusion ($16,000 in 2022).

There are many strategies used to reduce the estate and income taxes owed by deceased persons. While they are complex, they are needed to avoid unnecessary tax payments that can be lawfully avoided with a carefully executed estate plan.

PRINCIPLE TWO: Avoiding Probate

Although the threshold to avoid estate tax is high, the threshold to avoid the courts is very low. (See Chapter 16 for state-by-state probate limits). Probate court is not an evil monster waiting to steal all your assets at the end of your life. However, it also is not you. Probate is the judicial process designed to value your estate, name an executor and legally transfer assets in your estate to designated beneficiaries. A will, if it exists, is the guiding document. The judicial process, if necessary, is open to challenges, and the court will interpret a decedent's intentions.

— *What happens in probate*

This is a judicial process governed by state laws and legal precedence. A probate judge will determine whether the will is valid and appoint an executor. The executor will be in charge of gathering all the assets and necessary documents, then distributing them in the manner dictated by the will. The court will supervise the executor's progress and determine when the estate can be legally closed.

This all takes time and, depending on the state, the costs are borne by the estate. Probate fees vary considerably from state-to-state. Many states have adopted the Uniform Probate Code and limit fees to what is "reasonable" while other states like Florida still allow a probate attorney to charge a flat percentage of the estate's value.

— *Why things might move slowly in probate* —

Beyond the normal bureaucratic burden, there is the common problem of rounding up all the documentation and notifying all heirs. In some cases, legal heirs may be missing, incapacitated or non-responsive.

A notice of death must be published to potential creditors for a period of time and assets are typically frozen during the creditor claims period. The duration of the creditor claims period varies dramatically by state. Court filings are necessary for virtually every step of the process, requiring the attorney to coordinate with the judge's schedule, which tends to add additional time delays and inefficiencies. Consider what happened during the 2020 coronavirus pandemic when courts were closed for long periods of time, delaying the opening, administration and closing of probate estates and creating a significant backlog for probate judges.

In addition, there is always the problem of legal heirs who decide to contest the will. The probate process often makes it advantageous for legal heirs to try to get the will judged invalid under the intestacy laws, which are the laws that dictate who is entitled to inheritance.

Consider Ron who had three sons and a considerable estate. Two of the sons were upright citizens, close to Ron throughout his life. But the third became addicted to drugs and was a constant financial drain. During his lifetime, Ron spent over $250,000 on this son's addiction treatment and watched helplessly as valuable paintings and jewelry mysteriously disappeared from his home to pay for this son's addiction. When setting up his will, Ron divided his estate between the first two sons and left nothing to the third. It would certainly be in the third son's interest to contest the will as a legal heir and demand his third of the estate. He may or may not succeed, but the effort will prove both costly and time-consuming for the other two brothers.

— *How an estate ends up in probate*

There are many ways an estate can end up in probate or protracted litigation. Some of the more common ways include:

- A person dies intestate, meaning without a will
- A person has set up trusts that are either not valid or have not been properly funded, and the amount in the individual's name at death is in excess of the probate threshold
- A trust is challenged due to validity, capacity, fraud or undue influence
- Real estate is owned in the name of the person who passed

In some instances, attempts were made to distribute assets in accordance with a revocable living trust, but not all of the assets were properly retitled into the trust. Like anything else, estate planning must be well-executed to do what it is intended to do. If not, the desires of others will have their day in court and other people's motives do not always match yours.

— *Property in different states means multiple probates*

Real estate can pose particular problems when going through probate. Since probate courts in one state do not have jurisdiction in another, an executor can often find themselves engaged in two or more probate actions at the same time.

Say that Edward dies and leaves his homes in Illinois and Florida to his wife, Edna. Edna becomes sole owner of both properties and continues to enjoy her snowbird life, spending summers in her hometown where she can visit her children and grandchildren every day. When the winter winds turn cold, she climbs aboard a flight to Miami with only a small suitcase. There she spends the winter among her many friends on Singer Island in a large home she and Edward purchased many years before he died.

In Edna's will she nominated her eldest daughter, Claire, to be executor of her estate. Edna's property in Illinois will go through what is called "domiciliary probate" in her home state. At the same time, a second probate court action called "ancillary probate" will need to take place in Florida. The dual processes often require different local attorneys and will be longer, more complex and more expensive than a single probate action.

A well-executed and fully funded trust would have created a much simpler transfer to Edna's heirs while preserving the full value of the estate.

PRINCIPLE THREE: Protect Assets

Two things can sharply erode the value of an estate: taxes and creditors. Taxes, we've discussed. Some professions like doctors, attorneys and real estate developers are often the target of lawsuits. But in today's litigious society, everyone can be a target. Your surviving spouse may become involved in an unfortunate traffic accident and be subject to a large judgment. Perhaps a family company becomes ensnarled in a substantial legal judgment in a foreign country. Or consider the situation where a future ex-spouse (your son's ex-wife) wants to make a claim for maintenance or alimony. All can seriously erode an estate you took a lifetime to build and threaten the future happiness of those you want to take care of.

Insurance can often play a critical role in paying creditors and providing asset protection. The other protection available to you is to get the assets out of your name and into some form of an irrevocable trust.

During your lifetime, revocable trusts do not offer any protection from creditors since the assets are still considered under your control. However, a revocable living trust becomes irrevocable upon your death. This makes sense because, after you are gone, you don't want anyone else changing the terms of your trust. Generally, while a revocable living trust provides no asset protection during your lifetime, it can be structured so that the assets you leave to beneficiaries are protected from your creditors.

— *Asset protection trusts*

A handful of states, such as Wyoming, Nevada and South Dakota, will allow you to create a self-settled irrevocable trust (an irrevocable trust for the benefit of yourself). However, most state courts have found that the sole purpose to create an irrevocable trust for your personal benefit would be to evade creditors, which is against public policy.

Typically, irrevocable trusts refer to gift trusts created for a child or spouse. They are asset protected from creditors and often move assets outside of your taxable gross estate.

— *Leaving money to minor children*

Children and money seldom play well together. Even large estates can be dissipated by beneficiaries who don't know what they are doing with money. When assets pass to minor children, you want to make sure you protect the children not only from outside creditors — but also from themselves. You probably wouldn't want a child beneficiary to be able to go to the bank and withdraw a few million dollars on her 18th birthday. A trustee, or group of trustees, are appointed to manage the money in accordance with the terms of the trust. The trust may dissolve when the child reaches a set age or it may continue indefinitely with disbursements as needed.

When assets pass to minor children, you want to make sure you protect the children not only from outside creditors — but also from themselves

For obvious reasons, money left to minor children should always be left in a trust. However, there's more to consider than their care before they become adults. First, consider who you want to act as trustee over a children's trust. A beloved sister may be loved by your children and provide the perfect home for young children who have just lost their parents. However, she may also be a terrible money manager, dogged by debts and perpetually short of cash. It is probably a better idea to appoint another family member, friend or financial institution to act as a trustee who will be responsible for managing your children's financial affairs and making sure they are financially secure as they complete their educations and head into adulthood.

You should recognize that your children will all have different needs as they grow to maturity. By having them share in a single trust, you are essentially having the other children fund one child's medical school aspirations. To avoid this problem, you can divide the trust money into shares, with each owning their own shares with the ability to take money from their share as needed — or select an age at which the money should be divided. Many parents want everything to sit in one trust until the youngest child reaches age 21 and then divide. You can imagine a situation whereby the parent(s) may have helped the older kids by subsidizing undergraduate educations but the younger child did not get that benefit. By keeping everything in a single trust until the youngest child reaches 21, all of the children have an equal opportunity for college before the assets divide into separate but equal trusts for the kids.

When thinking about whether or not to allow children to withdraw money from the trust, and at what age, consider that, once withdrawn, the money becomes theirs. This means it will become available to creditors and will also be comingled with marital property in the case of a divorce. If you have any fear about your children's ability to manage money or their potential for divorce, especially without a prenuptial agreement, you should probably consider keeping the money in trust for future generations.

The same philosophy applies to problem children. Giving children access to large sums of money, even in adulthood, is playing with fire if there are any emotional, addiction or immaturity issues. A lifetime trust will help you protect your children from themselves while protecting the value of your estate for future generations to enjoy.

If you are confident in your children's ability to manage the money you leave them, you still may not want to turn it all over to them at a certain age. In these instances, people may choose to turn it over to them in managed stages. Many clients elect to give children "rights of withdrawal" or ownership over the assets upon reaching certain ages. Perhaps one-third of the trust at age 25, another third of the trust at age 30 and the remainder at age 35.

However, over time we have moved away from this type of distribution schedule for two primary reasons. First, the courts have found that if a beneficiary has an automatic right to trust assets upon reaching a particular age, asset protection is lost. Asset protection is not just against third-party creditors, but also a future ex-spouse trying to make a claim for maintenance or alimony. Second, because the child has these automatic rights, the IRS determines that the child has so much ownership and control over the funds, they are included in the child's taxable gross estate. Although few children may be concerned with a taxable gross estate, we don't know what a child's future net worth will be — or what the estate tax laws will be.

Instead of granting children such automatic rights of withdrawal, consider keeping assets in trust. This allows the inheritance to remain asset protected and structured so that the trust can qualify as being GST exempt, and pass estate tax free from generation to generation. In the same respect, we do not want to maintain control from the grave in perpetuity so select an age at which the child can become a co-trustee — or sole trustee of their separate trust. Because the child has the ability to access the trust assets in his or her discretion, as trustee, the assets remain asset protected and can qualify for maximum wealth transfer with GST planning.

— *What happens if a child dies?* —

When you set up the trust to take care of your children, you should also consider what should happen if something were to happen to them before they take ownership of the money. You could easily direct that the money will go to their children, if there are any, or that their share is distributed equally to your remaining children.

Often, people give their children special powers to direct

where the money goes long after you die. These "powers of appointment" give children the flexibility to direct trust money to their heirs (relatives) or charity when the time comes. In this manner, they make the determination of how trust money is used to benefit the next generation. The power of appointment can also be limited to descendants, helping to ensure the money passes to children and grandchildren, rather than spouses or in-laws. Or, if you wish to have the funds pass to a specific individual or charity that can be dictated as well.

— *Other threats to your assets* ————————————

You also have to consider dumb things that could happen to your money when you're gone. Money you expected would be used to care for your children and other beneficiaries.

Consider the case of a young couple, Edward and Phyllis, who had two young sons. Tragically, Edward was killed in a hiking accident. Fortunately, he had a $2 million insurance policy purchased with the hope of caring for both Phyllis and their small children by replacing the income they would lose if he died.

Unfortunately, Edward's death sent Phyllis into an emotional tailspin and soon the pool boy ended up with almost all the money.

However, if Edward had chosen to have the insurance payout made to a trust with his brother as trustee, the kids and Phyllis could have been well cared for, and the trust could even have paid for professional counseling to help Phyllis get through a very rough time — and ensure that, upon Phyllis' death, the balance passed to the children, as Edward would have intended.

— *Using insurance to protect asset value* —

At the very beginning of this chapter, we discussed what happens when insurance payouts expand the size of your estate, sometimes even pushing it over state and federal exemption levels. However, insurance can also play an invaluable role in protecting your family's future and protecting the overall value of your assets.

No matter the size of your estate, there are costs involved in transferring assets, paying funeral expenses and making sure dependents are cared for in the future. How are they going to replace your income? Will there be enough money to help the children go to college? How will a business maintain the capital necessary to carry on? How will heirs with special needs get the

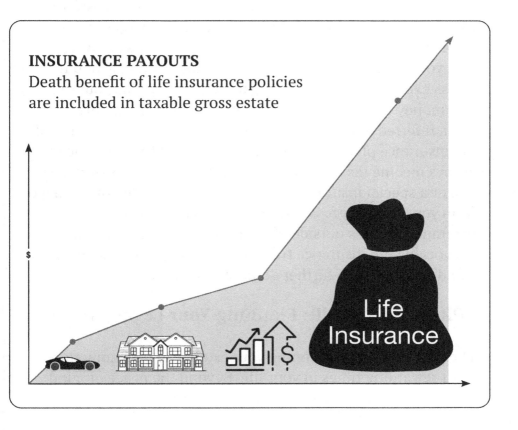

INSURANCE PAYOUTS
Death benefit of life insurance policies are included in taxable gross estate

care they require? These costs can substantially erode the value of your entire estate.

Insurance can play an important role in providing income-tax-free money to cover tax settlements, pay debts, provide needed support for survivors and protect asset value. Beneficiaries can use the full amount to pay asset transfer and funeral expenses, taxes, estate debts, medical costs, daily living expenses or anything else they will need. This may be especially important if you have a special needs child or relative. An insurance plan can be set up to make sure there is enough tax-free money available to take care of, or at least defray, costs for their future care.

In short, insurance can provide a needed boost to an estate's value. However, it can also be a boon to large estates above state and federal exemption limits. In these cases, knowing that your estate faces a large estate tax bill, you may find it is less expensive to purchase insurance that will pay out tax-free money to cover, or at least defray, estate taxes. This is often referred to as estate tax replacement. A critical aspect of life insurance planning is to understand that the insurance is always income tax free – but depending on how it is owned (by you or a special insurance trust) it may be included or excluded from your taxable gross estate. If you wish to move your life insurance policies outside of your taxable gross estate, an irrevocable life insurance trust (ILIT) is often recommended. We will discuss ILITs in further detail in Chapter 6.

PRINCIPLE FOUR: Planning Your Legacy

The time you spend planning your estate can be among the most rewarding times in your life. Beyond the peace of mind you'll gain by taking care of your family, this is also a time to reflect on your passions and decide what kind of legacy you'd like to leave behind. Where can some of the assets you've accumulated do the most good? How can the money you've accumulated during a lifetime of work support your passions long after you're gone? Leaving a legacy means making a difference beyond your life.

In this endeavor you'll find the government to be an ally, encouraging philanthropy and altruism with favorable tax treatments. Again, a special type of trust is the key to maximizing the altruistic power of your assets and minimizing taxes. As an ancillary benefit, charitable trusts allow you to see your money doing good while you're still alive.

— *Charitable planning and trusts*

Charitable planning can play a material role in your overall estate plan — and minimize your estate tax liabilities.

Charitable trusts are set up to benefit a charity or organization near and dear to your heart while providing an income tax deduction during your lifetime and minimizing estate taxes. With a charitable remainder trust, funds can be available to you during your lifetime with the remainder passing to charity upon your death. With a charitable lead trust, funds are used first by the charity for a period of time and then pass to designated family members.

For a more thorough look at charitable planning, see Chapter 12.

— *Managing charitable funds*

If you have a passion, but not a specific charity to support, you may prefer to set up a donor-advised fund with a local broker dealer or community foundation or even one managed by a local charity. Here you will find professionals skilled at both managing your assets and linking them with the kind of organizations you would like to support.

Funds managed by these organizations can be donor-advised, endowments, scholarships, field-of-interest funds, giving circles and more. The wide range of different fund opportunities makes it possible for even small estates to make a difference in their communities. Giving circles are an especially effective way to magnify small gifts. In these funds, individuals pool their money and jointly decide where to give money.

By working with local nonprofits or a community foundation, you can make sure your charitable gifts are being used where they are most needed in your local community.

— *Legacy means more than charity* —————————

Legacy planning does not have to deal solely with charitable issues. Take a broader view and realize that legacy planning is really about giving your estate plan a purpose beyond minimizing taxes and avoiding probate.

Perhaps the thing most important to you is to make sure future generations of your family earn college degrees. Maybe you want to maintain family ownership of a treasured property, business or art collection. Adopting a legacy viewpoint during your estate planning process can help you select the right tools to make your legacy dreams a reality.

Chapter 4
The Evolution of Marital Trusts

Trusts remain the key to maximize the assets you can pass on to the next generation or organizations you want to support.

However, there has been a recent evolution in the way trusts are structured to minimize taxes and maximize the value of the estate you pass on. In the days before estate tax exemptions rose to today's levels, there was a traditional way of structuring trusts known as "A/B trusts."

- **"A" Marital Trust:** Funded with everything in excess of the first spouse's available exclusion. The surviving spouse is the only beneficiary.

- **"B" Family Trust:** Funded with an amount equal to the unused portion of the first spouse's federal exemption. Beneficiaries may include the surviving spouse, the surviving spouse and children or just children.

The theory was fairly simple, but very dry, so let's liven it up by turning to my favorite fictional married couple: Brad Pitt and me. A girl can dream.

Traditional A/B Trusts

First, let's say Brad has a revocable living trust worth $15.06 million. Upon Brad's death, all of the assets received a step-up in basis to fair market value. Following his death, a portion of his assets worth the full estate tax exemption of $12.06 million were placed in his family trust, labeled the "B" trust. This is often called the credit shelter trust or a family trust/residuary trust. The credit shelter trust could be held for the benefit of the surviving spouse (me!), the children or the surviving spouse and children. What's most important to note about the credit shelter trust is that the assets pass estate tax free upon Brad's death and remain excluded from my taxable gross estate to pass estate tax free on my subsequent death. The assets in the credit shelter trust will receive a step-up in basis to fair market value on Brad's death and will subsequently pass to our children when I die. When that day arrives, the full amount in this credit shelter trust, including any appreciation, will pass free of federal estate taxes to our children.

In the meantime, the $3 million in assets Brad owned in excess of the federal estate tax exemption were placed in the A trust, designated a marital trust. I am the sole beneficiary. The marital trust assets are available for my needs and are included in my taxable gross estate. If I spend the money during my lifetime,

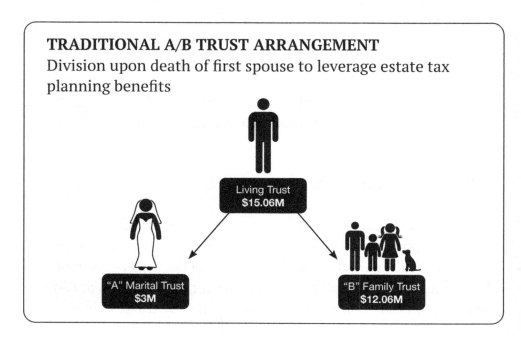

TRADITIONAL A/B TRUST ARRANGEMENT
Division upon death of first spouse to leverage estate tax planning benefits

Living Trust
$15.06M

"A" Marital Trust
$3M

"B" Family Trust
$12.06M

there is no estate tax owed on the $3 million in Brad's marital trust. Once again, in order to qualify as a marital trust, the assets can either be given to me outright, can remain in trust with me having a general power of appointment over the assets, or they can be held in a QTIP trust.

As a result, no estate tax was owed upon Brad's death.

A few years later, I died. (I'm certain it was due to a broken heart.) My living trust was worth $6.5 million on the day I died. The assets in my living trust and the remaining assets in Brad's marital trust are included in my taxable gross estate.

When Brad's family trust (or B trust) passes to our children, they are subject to income tax on the appreciation of those assets from Brad's date of death until mine. However, income taxes of 20% plus 3.8% Medicare taxes are not so bad if you are avoiding a 40% estate tax.

Let's say that Brad died at the beginning of a pretty good real estate and stock market run and his assets placed in the A and B trusts increased in value by 28% in the two years between our deaths. The marital trust is now worth $3.84 million, an increase of $840,000. The family trust is now worth $14,592,000, an increase of $3,192,000.

The B trust was never in my control so, although its assets stepped-up in value upon Brad's death, they do not get a second step-up in basis upon my death. Capital gains taxes will be owed on the $3,192,000 in appreciated value. At a tax rate of 20% plus 3.8% in Medicare taxes, almost $760,000 will be taken from our children's inheritance.

The value of the marital A trust is now worth $3.84 million

and is added to the $6.5 million in my living trust to bring the total value of my estate to $10.34 million on the day I died. The assets included in my estate (Brad's marital trust A and my assets) receive a step-up in basis to fair market value at the time of my death so no income taxes are owed. This is below my federal estate tax exemption level of $12.06 million in 2022, so it passes to my children free of federal estate and income taxes. Neither of our estates owed federal estate taxes.

There is an estate tax benefit to having the B trust assets pass outside of the surviving spouse's estate, but the cost is the loss of a second step-up in basis on the appreciation of assets during the time between the first spouse's death to the surviving spouse's death.

Either the income tax side goes up while the estate tax side goes down or the income tax goes down while the estate tax side goes up. Remember the teeter-totter.

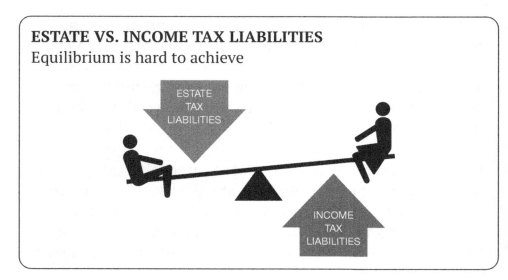

ESTATE VS. INCOME TAX LIABILITIES
Equilibrium is hard to achieve

For estates not threatened by federal or state estate taxes, income taxes, especially in the form of capital gains taxes, have become the bigger threat as federal estate tax exemption levels rise. Depending on the state you live in, there could also be major concerns with state estate taxes. Massachusetts and Oregon's state exemptions are only $1 million, an amount well within reach of middle-class households, especially with soaring home prices in parts of each of those states.

First, a little history. At the turn of the century, states received a credit on the total federal estate taxes paid. This credit was standardized and established by a table in the federal estate tax return instructions. Most states simply charged a state estate tax equal to the amount in the table. However, this credit was eliminated in 2001 and those states whose state estate tax rates were tied to the federal credit saw their state inheritance taxes essentially eliminated.

Estate planning has taken a turn from estate tax minimization to income tax minimization

In order to maintain necessary tax income, many states set up their own state estate and inheritance tax system. This became known as decoupling and the decoupled exemption level was often lower than the exemption level for federal estate taxes, especially after the federal ceiling was raised. So, while very few Illinois residents will leave estates valued above the federal estate tax exemption of $12.06 million in 2022, many more will leave estates valued above the Illinois state estate tax exemption of $4 million. For those with estates between $4 million and $12.06 million, the tax can be in excess of $1 million owed to the state of Illinois.

With the increased estate tax exemption, for many the threat of federal estate taxes was easing and the fear of state estate taxes and income taxes rising. Estate planning has taken a turn from estate tax minimization to income tax minimization.

Consider how the traditional A/B trust is changing to mitigate state level estate taxes.

Using QTIP Trusts in A/B Trusts

Another type of trust structure could help defer estate taxes and also ensure your children or preferred beneficiaries eventually inherit your assets. This is a "qualified terminable interest property" (QTIP) or the "A" trust in an A/B trust arrangement. As discussed on Page 57, this type of trust provides income for the surviving spouse while protecting the inheritance of other beneficiaries, perhaps the decedent's children from a previous relationship. Under a QTIP trust, the surviving spouse, providing he or she is a U.S. citizen, must receive income from the assets. Distributions of principal are often discretionary but can be customized for the surviving spouse's needs. When the surviving spouse dies, the principal and any unused interest is passed to the designated beneficiaries.

In the case where the surviving spouse is not a U.S. citizen, a qualified domestic trust (QDOT) can be used to implement the same strategy.

The only drawback to the QTIP trusts is that an estate tax return must be filed in order for the surviving spouse to make the QTIP election. However, if you rely on a fully funded marital trust, as described in the following pages, you may also want to file an estate tax return to capture portability.

QTIP SUB-TRUSTS

How used to decrease state estate taxes if your state allows for QTIP-elections

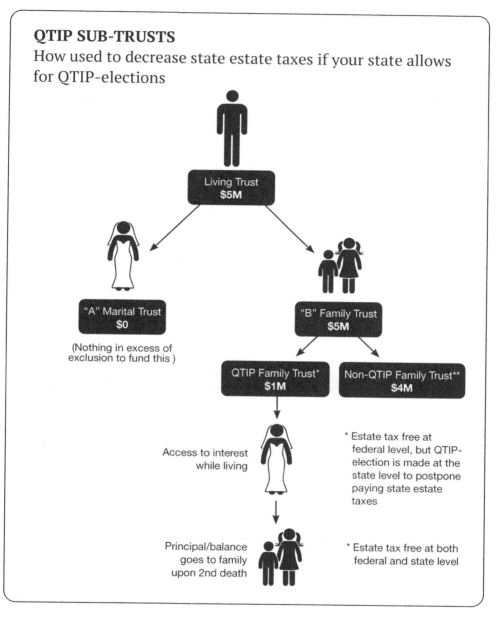

Consider the following situation. If Brad died with a gross estate of $5 million, I, as his surviving spouse, would not have to worry about federal estate taxes, but I would be very worried about

Illinois state taxes on the $1 million above the state exemption level of $4 million.

When setting up his estate plan, Brad had two major concerns: (1) he wanted to make sure I was well taken care of, and (2) he wanted to make sure his children from a previous marriage saw the inheritance he had planned for them even if I remarried.

Here's how he could plan his estate to minimize state estate taxes, take care of his surviving spouse, and ensure the money eventually makes its way to the children from his first marriage.

1. An amount equal to the state estate tax exemption limit is placed in the credit shelter trust. For Brad, who resides in Illinois, this is $4 million.

2. Anything remaining above that amount is placed in a second credit shelter trust which makes a QTIP election for state level purposes only. In Brad's case this would be $1 million. This amount would be estate tax free at the federal level but subject to Illinois estate tax. However, the tax is deferred until I die. (Not all states with estate taxes allow for QTIP elections at the state level.)

3. As Brad's wife, I have access to the funds in the QTIP. If I use all the money, the Illinois tax is never owed or paid.

4. The principal and any other money remaining in the QTIP passes on to Brad's children when I die.

When I die, my estate will consist of my revocable living trust plus the assets left to me from Brad's marital trust. It will be divided in the same manner as Brad's was to further minimize taxes due. To the extent my estate is subject to estate tax at the

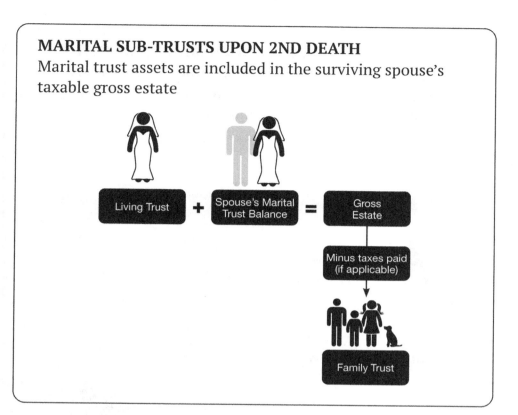

MARITAL SUB-TRUSTS UPON 2ND DEATH
Marital trust assets are included in the surviving spouse's taxable gross estate

Living Trust **+** Spouse's Marital Trust Balance **=** Gross Estate

Minus taxes paid (if applicable)

Family Trust

federal or state level, my estate or trust would pay the taxes. Thereafter, the balance would pass in trust for the benefit of our children. The remaining amount of money in the credit shelter QTIP trust would pass to the children from Brad's previous marriage as he intended. The trust allows for Brad to control the flow of funds from beneficiary to beneficiary.

Fully Funding the Marital Trust

Where a married couple is not concerned with estate tax liabilities, the focus shifts to minimizing potential income taxes for children. For this type of planning, we put all of the assets into the marital trust. This works if the total gross estate is less than both the federal and state exemption level. However,

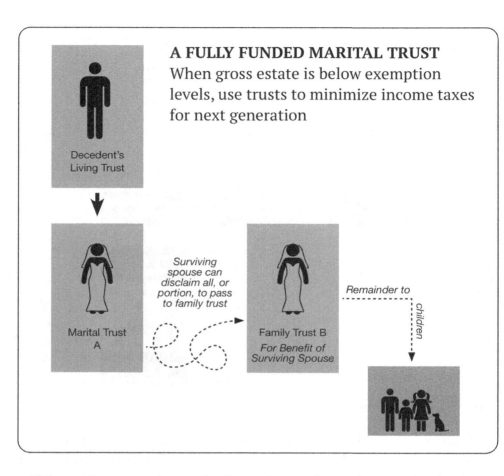

A FULLY FUNDED MARITAL TRUST
When gross estate is below exemption levels, use trusts to minimize income taxes for next generation

Decedent's Living Trust

Marital Trust A

Surviving spouse can disclaim all, or portion, to pass to family trust

Family Trust B
For Benefit of Surviving Spouse

Remainder to

children

if the assets grow dramatically or the tax laws change, they may potentially be subject to estate tax at a rate of 40%! The solution here is to build flexibility into the estate plan, allowing the surviving spouse to push part, or all, of their interest in the marital trust into the traditional credit shelter, or B, trust. This works to take an amount up to the exemption level and remove it from the surviving spouse's estate. In this planning scenario, we can decide if we want everything to sit in the marital trust or just a portion. As the surviving spouse, I have nine months from Brad's date of death to "disclaim" all or a portion of what is left to me in the marital trust to pass to the family trust. In doing so, I am also the beneficiary of the family trust, but the preference for which sub-trust is guided by tax planning priorities.

Plan for the Unthinkable

Many people think "that won't happen to us." But the reality is that stuff happens and life is not always as neat and tidy as we would like. Part of a good estate planning attorney's job is to imagine what disasters could befall a couple and steer them toward calm waters.

No one likes to think about the possibility of both partners dying in the same auto crash, yet it happens every day to rich, middle class and poor people alike. John F. Kennedy Jr. and Carolyn Bessette-Kennedy were young, famous and rich when they died together in a small plane crash. Apparently, Carolyn did not even have a will. In cases like these, assets held as joint tenants, or assets set up to pass to a surviving spouse, do not measure up to the couple's estate planning needs. Fortunately, John Jr.'s family was well-versed in estate planning needs, and the beneficiaries of his estate, valued between $30 and 100 million, were set up under the terms of a 1983 trust. He had updated these beneficiaries on a regular basis as the assets passed to his sister's children, various treasured friends, employees and associates, as well as charities near and dear to his heart.

Thinking through contingencies makes it easier to plan for the unexpected

Estate planners are often put in the unenviable position of talking to a married couple about the possibility of one spouse dying and the other remarrying. It is an important consideration, especially if they want to make sure that other dependents or charities are properly taken care of.

In the end, thinking through contingencies makes it easier to plan for the unexpected and protect the people and organizations you care about the most.

SECTION 2

Life Events that Affect Estate Planning

Every working day I sit in my office and talk to people about their lives. We talk about relationships, marriage, children, sometimes divorce, growing up and growing older with grace and hope. We discuss dreams, disappointments, expectations and surprises. Every life has a unique story that is woven with mystery, comedy and drama all rolled into one.

Every chapter brings a good estate plan into sharper focus. Relationships change. Financial circumstances change. Children grow up. Families grow. Inheritances get passed on. Laws change. A good estate plan is dynamic and changes over time with you.

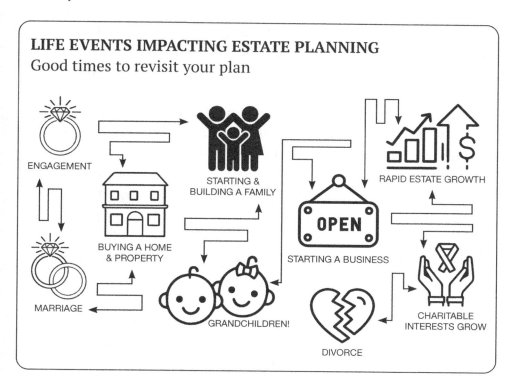

LIFE EVENTS IMPACTING ESTATE PLANNING
Good times to revisit your plan

ENGAGEMENT

STARTING & BUILDING A FAMILY

RAPID ESTATE GROWTH

BUYING A HOME & PROPERTY

STARTING A BUSINESS

MARRIAGE

GRANDCHILDREN!

DIVORCE

CHARITABLE INTERESTS GROW

There are a variety of life events that mark a turning point for estate planning needs:

- Getting engaged
- Getting married
- Buying a home and accumulating property
- Building a family
- Having grandchildren
- Starting a business
- Growing estates
- Increasing passion for charities
- Getting divorced

Every one of these events changes your relationship to the assets you've accumulated. As time passes there will be changes to your list of beneficiaries, how they are to be treated, and how tax and inheritance laws affect your plans for passing your estate to others. There will also be changes in your own thinking concerning how you would like the estate you built to benefit family, friends and charitable organizations.
In this next section we'll explore some of the most important estate planning issues that take place during each of these life-changing events. Let's have a bit of fun with a mythical couple whose life touches on all of these life events. As an ode to John Cougar Mellencamp, I'm going to share with you a little story about Jack and Diane. While they grew up in America's heartland, they are not kids. Rather, they reflect current trends nationally and delayed marriage until later in life. During those dating years, they move in together and have fulfilling careers. Jack is industrious, and he's been able to accumulate a substantial amount of wealth before tying the knot.

But really, Jack and Diane could be any of us. Maybe one or both of them are divorced, have kids or have parents with means. Or maybe Jack and Diane are really Jack and John or Diane and

Jocelyn. As we get to know Jack and Diane, we'll also consider some what-ifs — what changes when it comes to estate planning if their lives were somehow different.

Let's get to know the happy couple.

Chapter 5
Jack and Diane Get Engaged

Jack and Diane shared a special bond through high school and, when Jack left to attend Indiana University, Diane followed and enrolled in nursing school. Jack was studying finance because he felt that if you wanted to make money, you have to go where the money is. Their love blossomed and, right after graduation, they moved to Chicago and found a small basement apartment in Wrigleyville, just a few blocks from where Jack's beloved Cubs play.

Jack scored a job at a global investment banking firm and Diane settled into life at a private OB/GYN clinic. Diane spent many hours alone while Jack worked late, and she found herself wondering if there was room in Jack's ambitious career plans for her and the family she hoped to have some day.

Things changed one May day when Jack asked her to take the afternoon off to attend a Cubs game. They were to meet at Murphy's Bleacher's, a sports bar across from the field, for drinks before the game. Diane could not remember Jack ever spontaneously taking a day off and she feared something was wrong.

Upon arriving at Murphy's, she found a spot along the bar. She waited...and waited. Jack came strolling in too late for drinks, quickly flashed a pair of tickets behind home plate, threw down a $50 bill and hustled her out into the bright spring sunshine. They settled into their seats where, among other die-hard fans, they basked in the warm spring rays as they enjoyed the game.

It was the middle of the fourth inning when Diane turned around to look for the beer vendor that she felt the fans stirring. Thinking something was happening in the game, she instinctively looked at the large centerfield scoreboard and saw:

DIANE, WILL YOU MARRY ME??

The words streamed across the giant video screen just above a familiar man's face kneeling in front of a startled woman. She looked down and there was Jack, holding a small ring box in his hands. There, with 29,000 of their closest friends looking on, Jack was asking Diane to marry him. She enthusiastically said yes.

A new life, together, began.

To Prenup or Not to Prenup ... That is the Question

Couples in love often express concern that negotiating a prenuptial agreement will cause their relationship to sour. In my experience, that has never been the case. Too often, couples romanticize the relationship and fail to recognize the financial implications associated with marriage — and a potential divorce. A prenuptial agreement is not planning for a divorce. Rather, it is an opportunity to make certain you are on the same page as you move forward toward building a life together. It is how you address what would be equitable in the event things are not happily ever after. If a prenup is appropriate, it is best to develop one quickly, and then focus on the fun parts of engagement and marriage.

In order to determine if a prenuptial agreement makes sense for you, I encourage people to sit down with an attorney to get a feel for their rights and options before addressing this with a partner. This allows you to be educated on your options and the nuances for your specific situation.

In many ways a prenup can be anything you want it to be. Most of all it is a legal document detailing how assets will be owned during the marriage and divided in the event of divorce. However, a good prenuptial agreement also addresses what happens upon death. The prenup sets the minimum amounts partners intend to leave to each other, leaving partners the option to leave more, which is often the case in long love-filled marriages.

Unless otherwise specified, assets accumulated before the marriage are characterized as individual or non-marital assets. Those accumulated during the marriage are marital assets, subject to division according to state law (or as detailed in the prenuptial agreement). Since the prenup details how these assets will be divided in the event the marriage ends, it is better to make decisions when you're in love and can think rationally. Too often, after things go south, those decisions are harder to make fairly.

A prenup can address virtually anything except anything related to children, which is against public policy. Child custody and child support are prohibited from being addressed. Prenups are also subject to state laws, so it matters greatly if you live in a community property state versus a common law state. (See Chapter 16 for a list of community property states).

Without a prenuptial agreement, the division of assets could well be at the mercy of state law. In some states Diane (or Jack) would be entitled to spousal support or maintenance, as well as 50% of all assets accumulated during the marriage. In other states, the division is determined by what the courts characterize as equitable. Many interpret equitable to mean equal, but that is rarely the case. In other words, a judge who knows nothing about you will have the last word. That's another reason why it is better to have a prenup negotiated between the partners during a happy, rational time in their relationship.

Avoiding Court with a Prenuptial Agreement

Once your estate, or divorce, ends up in court, you lose control, waste time and helplessly watch your hard-earned money dissipate in court costs and legal fees. A good prenuptial agreement offers a better way.

In order to be effective, a prenuptial agreement must be based on full-disclosure. It is a bit like getting naked in front of others and disclosing assets, liabilities and income. Depending on the financial situation of the couple involved, tax returns or business valuations may even be required. Each party must also have separate legal representation so neither can later claim they didn't know what they were signing.

A good prenuptial agreement offers a better way

If it's beginning to sound like an adversarial exercise, it shouldn't be. A prenuptial agreement never sabotages a wedding, although it may expose problems couples had on their own. It was just that the prenup forced the couple to address issues they hadn't yet communicated about as a couple. In these cases, a lost wedding leads to a happier life for both partners. A well-drafted prenuptial agreement protects everyone.

Finally, make sure that any professional working on your estate plan has a copy of the prenuptial agreement you both signed. A big part of the estate planning attorney's job is to keep you out of court, so any plan they help you develop must adhere to the terms of your initial agreement.

Consider the predicament currently facing Sally. She and David signed a prenuptial agreement with David bringing substantial assets and some baggage from a previous marriage into the relationship. David updated his estate plan fully intending to make sure Sally was well taken care of. However, he didn't show his attorney a copy of the prenuptial agreement and, consequently, his good intentions went awry.

The prenup provided that in the event of David's death, Sally would get $1 million outright, or to her in a trust which she could control. In his updated estate plan, David actually left her more, but placed the money in a trust she couldn't control. When David died, Sally found her money tied up in a trust controlled by a step-daughter with whom she had a difficult relationship. Going to court to enforce her rights would prove costly, time-consuming and would likely sever her relationship with family members. The drama could have been eliminated had David simply shared the prenuptial agreement with the estate planning attorney.

Watch Out for Comingling

Generally, absent a prenup, anything owned before marriage or gifted or inherited by one spouse during marriage is considered individual or non-marital property. Anything earned during the marriage is considered marital property. Many people then ask, "If the assets are already individual or non-marital, why would I need a prenup to protect them?" The issue is that it is easy for assets to be "tainted" or "transmuted" in the eyes of the law. These terms can be one in the same, but an individual or non-marital asset becomes tainted when it is muddled as a result of co-mingling it with marital assets. This can be done intentionally or through words, actions or contribution of marital assets. When an individual asset becomes a marital one, transmutation has occurred. Here's how co-mingling plays out in actual situations.

Let's say Jack has a passion for old cars and a knack for restoring them. Before getting married, he purchased a 1965 Mustang for $20,000 with the intention of fixing it up some day. Once married, Jack charged the parts needed to continue the restoration on their joint credit card that was paid from their joint bank account, and Diane spent a lot of time in the garage with him handing him tools and cleaning up messes. The Mustang is now worth $100,000, but it is also tainted. Diane could make the claim that it is marital property.

If Jack had only used pre-marital funds to buy everything needed for the restoration and did the project on his own, the Mustang could have remained an individual, non-marital asset. But by using marital funds to finance the restoration, the Mustang became tainted. A prenuptial agreement could have helped to further strengthen an argument that the asset would remain an individual, non-marital asset.

Perhaps Jack is a savvy investor and turned his car passion into a $2 million dollar investment account before marriage.

Without thinking, he automatically adds Diane to the account. His $2 million account has now been transmuted to joint ownership. Now, let's say Diane is as bad with money as Jack is good. She has managed to run up a $150,000 credit card debt and has a long-lost brother who desperately needs money. That investment account is now available to Diane's creditors, and Diane could choose to use a good chunk of Jack's pre-marital money to help her brother. Jack could be okay with this scenario but, more likely, he isn't.

Since both parties bring assets of some sort into a marriage, it is important to look at this ownership structure in advance to ensure anything you want to remain yours does. And that which you want to share with your new spouse is done so in a manner you both agree to.

A well-drafted prenuptial agreement helps partners look at the life before them and smooths the path they will walk together

It is better to have a prenuptial agreement, negotiated with professionals in the room, to determine what will become a marital asset and what remains non-marital. It is up to the parties to agree on what the terms of ownership are. Perhaps Jack doesn't want to share his hard-earned investment account until he knows the marriage is solid. Maybe he feels five years is a reasonable time to start sharing valuable assets accumulated before the marriage. Perhaps he wants to wait until there are children. The prenup can have a sunset clause saying when certain provisions of the agreement disappear, or sunset, and identify a point in time when the individual non-marital assets (or a portion thereof) will become marital.

A well-drafted prenuptial agreement helps partners look at the life before them and smooths the path they will walk together.

Life Happens

Jack and Diane could be any American couple starting a life together, and they could have very different concerns when sitting down to execute their first estate plan. Let's look at how a prenuptial agreement could affect Jack and Diane's estate planning needs depending on what twists and turns their lives might take.

— *Jack bought a big house before meeting Diane* —

He's the proud owner of a million-dollar co-op that represents a large part of his estate. Upon marriage, the co-op automatically becomes half owned by Diane if they live in a community property state. If they live in a common law state and the property is retitled to include her, Diane is entitled to her share. What many fail to recognize is that even if Jack doesn't retitle the house, it has the potential to become tainted or transmuted to a marital asset. Although Jack owned the home prior to marriage, in the eyes of the court, the house is benefiting the marital unit, opening the door to be tainted. In any case, Jack's estate has diminished while Diane's has grown. Perhaps this is the way they want their married life to start. Perhaps not.

Houses are one of the easiest assets to taint in this manner, and it's a compelling reason for people with real estate holdings to consider a prenup. If Jack didn't intend to diminish his estate so quickly, the prenuptial agreement could detail when the co-op would be considered marital property. Perhaps they feel that after seven years of marriage, the home Jack, alone, brought into the marriage would be co-owned.

— Diane is Jack's second wife —————————————

A previous marriage may mean children, debts or both. Jack may need to safeguard the ability of his children to inherit even as he starts a new life with another wife.

Key considerations are how to maintain an equitable distribution of assets when the time comes. If Jack simply adds Diane to all his accounts, giving her co-ownership, those accounts become Diane's property when he dies. She has complete control over how the assets are used now and who she will leave them to upon her death. If Jack wanted to make sure his children from his prior marriage inherited their rightful share, assets should have been placed in a trust with the children included as designated beneficiaries.

— Diane's father is rich —————————————————

In setting up a prenuptial agreement and estate plan, it helps to know what each partner expects to inherit. Perhaps Diane's father is a wildly successful manufacturer. As one of three children, she expects to eventually inherit quite a bit of money. The time before marriage is the perfect time to have a discussion about how this windfall will be handled.

Should it remain non-marital assets or become marital? Could Jack really be marrying Diane for her money? Who knows? However, it's a safe bet Diane's father wants the money to stay in the family. Although inheritance during the marriage is considered an individual, non-marital asset, consider what would happen if the inherited assets became marital property through inadvertent tainting. Perhaps Jack and Diane's marriage falters and they divorce or Diane dies first and Jack remarries. Suddenly a big chunk of the family fortune would become another family's good fortune.

In addition to addressing this in the prenup, the easiest way to protect inherited assets is to have Diane inherit them through an inheritance trust (discussed in Chapter 4). Diane would have access to the funds during her lifetime but, while they remain in trust, they would be asset protected from her creditors (including a future ex-spouse, like Jack, trying to make a claim for maintenance or spousal support).

— *Jack has a business*

Let's say Jack is part of a successful business from which he earns a salary. It could be a business run by his family for three generations or one he started himself. Without a prenuptial agreement, including a section on how Jack's interest is to be handled, his ownership could easily be transmuted. If their marriage was to end in divorce, Diane could always claim she helped him build the business by entertaining customers and employees entitling her to some ownership in his company.

Changes in ownership can often doom a business, especially if buyout clauses in partnership agreements would put an undue burden on the business or other partners. In situations like this, it is important to have a conversation before the marriage even begins to decide whether Jack's business interests are to be considered a marital or non-marital asset. Does Jack expect Diane to help out with the business? If so, will she have an interest? Will the interest be immediate or after a period of years?

In answering these questions, it is important to determine how vital it is for Jack to maintain control of either the business or his share of the business. When a family business is involved, other family members will have an interest in making sure Jack's ownership shares cannot be transmuted. By designating a pre-existing business as a non-marital asset, or protecting the business by placing shares in a trust, the business is protected.

— *Jack is suddenly out of the picture* —

As I said earlier, an important part of estate planning is to see possible trouble ahead. No one likes to think of tragedy, but life happens. What happens if Jack dies in a tragic accident one week after the wedding? Or perhaps he dies of a fatal disease within the first few years of married life. Maybe a deep, dark secret (I'll leave it to your imagination) rears its ugly head and the marriage ends a short time after it began.

In cases like this, Diane has to be protected in both the prenuptial agreement and estate plan. Maintenance and housing are going to be key issues. Diane won't want to be thrown out of the house she's living in, and she won't want to be left penniless through no fault of her own.

Again, communication is key. Perhaps Jack doesn't want Diane thrown out of their home, but he doesn't want his largest asset left to her family members. The house could be held in trust for Diane's benefit, protecting her ability to remain in the home and cover expenses. However, upon her death, the trust could provide that the asset then passes to Jack's intended beneficiaries.

Have the conversation, then decide on the plan that meets both people's needs and expectations.

Conversation Starters
Before Tying the Knot

If you are recently engaged, you'll want to make sure the two of you have a shared vision for your future family, as well as how finances will be managed. Here are some questions that will help you guide that conversation with your soon-to-be spouse. And in many instances, it may make sense to sit down with an attorney to ensure you are informed of your rights and understand the legal nuances before you have these conversations with a partner. The attorney can help advise you on how to broach the subject and identify key considerations for your particular situation.

1. **How do you feel about sharing any assets you are bringing into the marriage? Is there ever a time when I may have some ownership of them? If so, when?**
   Make sure you agree on what will become marital assets and the timeframe, if any, for it to happen. Perhaps the primary residence will become a "marital asset" after a fifth wedding anniversary.

2. **Do you have any debt? Whom do you owe and how much? Are all your payments current?**
   Have a clear understanding of the debts your partner is bringing into the marriage and if there is any situation where creditors may target your joint assets.

3. **Do you see us having a joint bank account or will our finances remain separate? Or will we each have a separate account as well as our joint account?**
   Agree on how your finances will be handled. Just because your parents did it one way doesn't mean you have to handle them in the same manner.

4. **How will our debts be paid? Do you think we should each pay our own way or will they be handled jointly? What about those assets, like a new dishwasher, that we will likely acquire jointly?**
It would be a good idea to discuss what each partner needs to feel financially secure in the relationship and, if that includes maintaining separate money, who will pay for new items.

5. **Do you think any of your family members would include you in their will? If so, what do you think you might inherit?**
Before marriage you should know if there is the possibility of a large inheritance that may cause problems or opportunities.

6. **When we have children, will we both continue to work? Or will one of us stay home to be the primary caregiver? What does that mean financially for the stay-at-home parent?**
Be clear about your career expectations if children come along. If one spouse expects to leave the workforce, how will they be taken care of if the marriage ends in divorce?

7. **What are your current financial commitments to support your children? If you were to unexpectedly pass away, what would you want them to inherit? Does that change if we have children together at the time?**
Make sure you both understand each other's previous entanglements and how your spouse expects to care for

dependents both during and after your marriage.

8. **Would you feel at all awkward about negotiating and signing a prenup? Do you know how this can protect both of us?**
    Talk about your feelings regarding prenuptial agreements. Make sure you understand the benefits of having one, especially if either of you have sizeable assets now. Remember, this isn't just divorce protection, but also death protection, so it is extremely valuable.

9. **If one of us were hit by a bus next year, what would happen to the other one? How could we ensure we were prepared and protected?**
    Since a prenup is effective upon marriage, it can provide for one another upon death until you have time to set up an estate plan. Know how you see current assets being distributed in that unfortunate instance.

10. **Where do we see ourselves living? Do you ever think we'd move to another state during our marriage?**
    Residing in a community property or common law state may have an impact on whether a prenup is necessary or recommended.

11. **Do you currently have an estate plan in place? What does it say now? When should we see about updating it?**
    If there is a current plan in place, it probably excludes the soon-to-be spouse and should be updated in light of your upcoming marriage.

Chapter 6
Jack and Diane Get Married

After a 14-month engagement, Diane stood in her bedroom surrounded by icons from her childhood. It was just like she left it, except for the wedding dress hanging in the closet. As she looked around, she was flooded with memories and wondered if this is how a young Diane pictured this day.

Diane gathered her gown and turned to find her father standing in the doorway with a wistful look in his eye. Growing up she never really knew what he was thinking but, somehow, she always knew he was thinking about her, and he always made sure she was okay. Together, they walked down the stairs, out the front door and along the concrete sidewalk to the waiting limousine. As they approached the church, a magnificent rainbow formed over the steeple, "just like in the movies," thought Diane. As she walked through the side door of the church, she saw her childhood friends, Debbie and Mary, looking like spring dressed in matching safflower bridesmaids' dresses. "This is really happening," she thought.

After getting in her dress and having pictures taken, Diane waited for the ceremony to start. Debbie and Mary tried to calm her nerves, but her mind was racing. She thought about the advice the minister had shared in their marriage classes to help ensure a happy marriage. She thought about Jack's rapidly growing career and how he was working so hard to build a life for the two of them. She thought about their house in Lincoln Park...the one Jack bought, but fought to keep as non-marital property in their prenup. None of that mattered right now as she would soon be Jack's wife.

With her arm in her father's, they made their way down an aisle lined by family and friends. Halfway down she saw Jack. Only 10 more steps and she'd arrive at her destination. The time had come for two to become one.

A Life Together Begins

Jack and Diane are finally ready to begin their lives together as one. Or are they? The fact is that modern marriages are not one size fits all. Some couples want to blend their physical and financial lives together. Others yearn to maintain separation while still working together as a team. A marriage is what you make of it.

If they adhered to the advice offered in the previous chapter, Jack and Diane will already have shared conversations about expectations and reflected these talks in their prenuptial agreement. However, now is the time to make sure some basic estate planning needs are in place. This becomes even more important if they didn't execute a prenuptial agreement.

Every marriage and relationship evolves, and Jack and Diane's will not be any different. From newlyweds, they will become parents and grandparents. Their financial circumstances will change greatly, as will their understanding of each other's needs and desires. As their lives change, so should their estate plan. Let's look at how some of these changes will play out from an estate planning perspective.

A Newlywed's Estate Planning Checklist

As a couple begins their life together, they need to address some key areas to ensure they are off on the right foot.

— *Ownership of assets*

If no prenuptial agreement is in place, you need to agree on how you want pre-marital and future marital assets to be owned. Is your vision of marriage share-and-share alike, or is your vision more along the lines of two individuals raising a family? Perhaps you feel it is best to maintain totally separate financial lives. Or, you may want to keep your premarital assets separate but share everything going forward. There is no right answer, only an answer that works for you as a couple. If one partner owns substantial pre-marital assets, it might be best to keep those titled in their name and in a separate trust with beneficiaries they designate.

It is never too early to plan for future estate taxes and division of assets in the event of divorce or death of one spouse. You also have to start considering how to protect any current or future assets from creditors or erosions due to taxes.

Again, if this has not been worked out in a prenuptial agreement, now is the time to visit your estate planning attorney and start building trusts to hold the assets you will accumulate together. If you want to keep assets accumulated before the marriage separate, it would be a good idea to start a trust strictly for those assets. This will allow the partner who accumulated the assets to make the final decision on the ultimate beneficiaries. It will all help you clearly delineate which assets are marital and which are individual in case the marriage hits stormy weather.

— *Planning for catastrophe* ————————————

It's hard to think about, but what happens if one spouse dies or becomes incapacitated. You both need to consider what it would take to financially support the other and provide proper care for the incapacitated spouse. Think about the financial resources available in case of catastrophe. Even if you have sizeable resources, it may be wise to purchase life insurance and disability insurance allowing you to handle an unexpected situation with tax-free dollars. The proceeds from the life insurance policies can be owned by and distributed to an irrevocable life insurance trust (ILIT) to make sure the money is protected from state or federal estate taxes.

The death benefits on any life insurance is included in your taxable gross estate if it is not placed in an irrevocable trust. If the combination of the other assets in your estate and the proceeds from the insurance policy puts the value of the estate over the state or federal exemption level, there will be substantial estate taxes to pay.

However, if you form an ILIT to either purchase or take ownership of the policy, the proceeds can pass estate tax free. You will not be able to serve as trustee or make any changes to the policy and beneficiaries during your lifetime or else the IRS would consider the policy under your control and part of your taxable estate. Your spouse or children can serve as trustees if you wish.

— *Understanding your future* ————————————

You may already have discussed your hopes for a future family. Now is the time to consider how to afford the family you'd like to raise. With college costs skyrocketing, it is never too early to start a college fund or to set up an educational trust. Soon after marriage, and before your family grows, is a good time to look into starting a 529 college fund to set aside tax-free dollars for future educational purposes.

— *Setting the stage for future financial security* —

Everyone hopes to be financially successful. Planning for it brings your hopes closer to reality. If you already have accumulated substantial assets, now is the time to consider how you can protect those assets and who you would like to benefit from them in the future.

Retitling Assets

As you drew up your pre-nuptial agreement, you decided how you want the assets each of you are bringing into the marriage to be owned. Depending on your combined views about marriage, you either maintained separate ownership or agreed to combine ownership upon marriage or sometime in the future. Now the time has come to turn those agreements into reality.

The devil is in the details, as they say, and simply agreeing to share assets means little unless you actually retitle them. You can go to all the expense of creating a living trust, but if you don't fund the trust by transferring assets into the trust, and updating beneficiary designations, it is all for naught. A trust is just an empty shell until you actually put assets in its name.

Simply agreeing to share assets means little unless you actually retitle them

Overlooking the simple retitling of assets has had dire consequences for people who came up with a great estate plan, but did not follow through with actually titling assets in the name of their trusts. If assets are not properly retitled and remain held as joint tenants with rights of survival, the assets would pass directly to a surviving spouse. In doing so, we lose the asset protection and wealth transfer opportunities of the trust. In addition, regardless of what the estate planning documents (or divorce decree) may say, beneficiary designations govern. So, if someone forgets to remove an ex-wife as a beneficiary of a retirement plan asset, it will still go to the ex-wife.

The funding of trusts and retitling of assets can be handled by your attorney. But often clients are interested in saving money and wish to handle it on their own. If you work with a financial planner or wealth advisor, the investment professionals should be able to help retitle investments and update beneficiary designations. However, real estate transfers and assignments of business interests should be handled by an attorney.

Since the prenuptial agreement does not take effect until the marriage takes place, retitling of assets should happen immediately after the wedding. Retitling a home can be done by drawing up a new deed in the name of the new owners and having it recorded with your local county auditor. If you are placing assets in a trust as part of your estate plan, often the trust becomes the new owner, but the real estate recommendations for your primary residence can vary dramatically based on the state in which you reside.

Some states offer asset protection for married couples for their primary residence by holding title as tenants by the entirety. Under tenants by the entirety, the asset is not deemed to be owned by either party — but rather by the couple as a fused marital unit. In this way, a creditor of either spouse cannot reach the asset — only a joint creditor of both spouses can go after the home. However, tenants by the entirety is not treated the same in every state. See the chart on Chapter 16 to see if tenants by the entirety is recognized in your state for real estate or all assets.

For example, Illinois allows you to hold title to a primary residence through your trusts, as tenants by the entirety, to get the best estate planning and asset protection. Michigan allows title to any real estate to be held as tenants by the entirety. Florida allows title to any asset (including investments) to be held as tenants by the entirety. This is why it is important for an estate planning attorney to guide you through the estate planning and asset protection nuances.

If there is a mortgage on the property, the mortgage holders may need to sign off on the change. This is not usually a problem, especially in the case of spouses taking joint ownership. Investment accounts and other assets can be retitled by changing ownership names of the account documents. Often times, financial institutions require a new account to be opened in the name of the trust and require the investments transferred in kind to the new account. By handling it in this way, the investments are not sold and then transferred, but rather the portfolio stays intact and transfers to the trust account.

Beneficiaries should also be updated on life insurance and retirement plan assets. If a prenup has been signed, beneficiaries of trusts and insurance policies should be examined and updated in accordance with the agreement. Remember, a living trust without assets or beneficiaries will not prevent assets from being thrown into probate. In order to leverage all of the benefits of your living trust, it must be funded.

Using Insurance to Meet Health and Financial Needs

This is a good time to think about how each of you would manage if something were to happen to the other. If one spouse is the breadwinner, how would the other take care of financial obligations if the breadwinner died or became incapacitated? Life insurance and disability insurance can provide tax-free income to fill holes in your financial plan. One or the other may have already purchased insurance, but beneficiary designations will have to change with the new marital status and estate planning.

Keeping Your Estate Plan in Line with New Familial Considerations

The conversation continues as long as you are married. Every time a change happens in your family, new estate planning concerns may arise. Perhaps children come along. Or maybe Diane's sister hits some hard luck and Diane wants to make sure she is taken care of if Diane should predecease her.

It is just as likely that, as Jack and Diane accumulate more wealth, estate taxes become a concern leading them to revise their estate plans to minimize tax bites if one or both of them die.

In one instance I know of, the husband owned a chain of lucrative car dealerships and was facing serious health problems. Over two decades he went through more than a dozen life-threatening surgeries. Before every surgery he and his wife sat down with their estate planning attorney to make sure their plan reflected the needs of their growing estate and maturing family. He considered having a good estate plan in place part of his parental and marital responsibilities.

Alternate Realities

New marriages today are diverse and many do not resemble a young, never-before-married Jack and Diane tying the knot. Many people choose to live together in committed relationships foregoing marriage. Let's look at what would be different in these alternative scenarios.

— *Diane married Jocelyn rather than Jack* —

Love is love. In June of 2015, the U.S. Supreme Court legalized same sex marriage. With same sex marriages recognized at the federal and state levels, many couples had new estate planning options open to them. The simple fact is that the sex of the partners no longer makes a difference when it comes to estate planning. Marriage equality is estate planning equality.

In many cases this means couples who could not previously marry now may elect to reconfigure their estate plans with new realities in mind. They may have previously shared a committed relationship, but committed and married are very different in the eyes of the law. Now they can enjoy both the tax and estate planning benefits only available to married couples.

At the time of the ruling, I had the privilege of working with two extraordinary women who suddenly had tax advantages available to them as a married couple that weren't available when they were simply living together in a committed relationship. One had an estate substantially over the federal exemption level. If she were to die as a single woman, every dollar over the exemption would be taxed. By marrying, they could take advantage of marital exemptions to double the amount of money they can shield from estate taxes and ensure that no estate tax is owed at the federal or state levels until both of them have passed away.

Couples like these two women may have had trusts drawn up for them as individuals that can now be reconfigured as A/B trusts (see Chapter 4) to minimize state and federal estate taxes while providing financial support for a surviving spouse.

— *Jack brought children into the marriage* —

What happens if either Jack or Diane were married before or have children from a previous relationship? The parental spouse may well want to be sure these children receive their full inheritance. Again, an A/B trust arrangement (see Chapter 4) will provide a way to guarantee that these children are provided for while also providing for the surviving spouse and any children Jack and Diane may have together.

— *Jack and Diane decide marriage is not for them* —

Despite the tax benefits of marriage, a couple may decide they are happier living together as separate individuals. Others decide they are quite happy living their life as a single person without any significant other. The beauty of today's world is there really is no right or wrong way to live your life. Estate planning is for everyone.

The beauty of today's world is there really is no right or wrong way to live your life

---

Estate Planning for Single People

It may seem odd to end a chapter on estate planning for married couples with a discussion of the same need for single people. An odd twist of modern life is that people seem to be getting married later in life, often when careers have already been built and assets accumulated. And, more and more people are having children and becoming single parents by choice.

Once you have assets (and kids), you need to have an estate plan in place. Certainly there are tax ramifications, but you will also find it incredibly empowering to recognize the assets you've acquired and assert control over where they go and the type of legacy you'd like to leave. Many single people also see themselves marrying in the future. In these cases, estate planning is a good vehicle to identify non-marital assets and get them into a separate trust.

If you are single and intend to stay that way, you still must plan to minimize estate taxes without the benefit of marital exemptions, joint gifting and other tax benefits available to married couples. Whether or not your estate exceeds the state and/or federal exemption level, you will certainly want to think about who you'd like to benefit from your assets when you pass on. You may be a single parent, or beneficiaries could include nieces, nephews or siblings. It could just as easily be treasured friends or organizations you've supported throughout your life.

Singles also need to understand what happens if they die younger than expected. Under intestate succession laws, if you are single with no children, everything will pass to parents who may well be in the process of passing their own wealth to the next generation. The addition of a child's estate to their own could have significant ramifications.

Every life stage puts the spotlight on different estate planning needs. However, whether single or married, we all share a need to maintain control of our hard-earned resources and a desire to help others. Estate planning is the tool to do both.

Conversation Starters
After the "I Do's"

Recently married couples have very similar conversations to newly engaged couples. After all, in both instances you are searching for ways to become a couple and define exactly what that means to each of you. The major difference is that upon saying "I do" it all becomes so much more real. Whether or not you both felt comfortable executing a prenuptial agreement, here are some things to talk about while still newlyweds.

1. **How will we handle titling homes and other things we acquire in the future?**
    The idea of ownership can be touchy. Make sure you are clear about the way houses, cars and more will be titled in the future. Also, make sure you both understand what the best titling strategy is for your future financial health.

2. **What happens if one of us earns more than the other? How would the gap be filled if something happened to the breadwinner?**
    When you first marry, it is hard to have a conversation about being separated, but life happens, and you'll want to make sure the surviving spouse has a certain standard of living. Having a plan in place will be of great comfort in the event of catastrophe.

3. **Should we look into buying life or disability insurance?**
    There are two good reasons for buying insurance: protection against catastrophe and adding tax-free dollars to your estate. Insurance may prove especially helpful in filling the

financial gap if something happens to a breadwinner.

4. **How will we pay for education, healthcare, etc. for our future children?**
   With college costs rising, it is never too early to start setting money aside. And private elementary and secondary education can be pricey, too.

5. **How do you think we should distribute those assets we accumulated before marriage when one of us dies?**
   With marriages taking place later in life, there are complications to modern life that need to be sorted out.

6. **Do you have a will or other estate planning tools already in place? If so, what do they say and when should we look at making revisions?**
   Estate plans executed when single will certainly need to be looked at from a married perspective. Be sure to review beneficiaries and make changes as needed.

7. **Should we talk to HR at work and make changes to the beneficiaries on our retirement, healthcare and other benefit plans?**
   This could very easily lead to a conversation about using trusts as beneficiaries.

8. **What will I need to do if I change my last name?**
   You may be surprised by the number of assets and beneficiary designations that should be changed as soon as possible.

9. **When should we put an estate plan in place?**

Too many people put estate planning on the back burner for far too long. It is a good idea to get this on your to-do list as quickly as possible, especially if either party has sizeable assets including real estate.

10. If one of us runs into some serious health problems, who's going to be responsible for making medical decisions?

Putting together a healthcare power of attorney is a good idea. You may be surprised at the peace of mind you'll both have with things like this out of the way.

11. If one of us died unexpectedly next year, what would happen to the other one? How could we ensure that we are prepared and protected?

Life happens, and it helps if you have a plan in place to hold and distribute assets with minimum loss from taxes. Also, make sure each of you know where your assets are, how they will be distributed, and any login and password details.

Chapter 7
Jack and Diane Start to Accumulate Assets

By the time Jack and Diane celebrated their third wedding anniversary, Jack had already left the large investment banking firm where he was on track to become a partner and formed a real estate investment partnership with his three best friends. The friends acquired three apartment buildings and a small oil and gas drilling business. They were growing something big and realized that it needed their full commitment.

While Diane saw little of Jack, who seemed to be working more and more, she certainly enjoyed the perks of a successful business. There had been thrilling vacations to Asia, Europe and even Northern Africa. From Paris to Budapest to Marrakesh, she saw more of the world than she ever dreamed she would.

Now with clients and investors to entertain, the bungalow Jack purchased before their marriage was starting to feel small. Diane was happy with their home, but understood Jack's desire for something more. She worked with one of Chicago's highest-flying realtors to find a wonderful home in Glencoe. It was a French provincial in an older, leafy neighborhood off Valley Road with exquisite architecture and dramatic spaces for entertaining. It was the ideal home for an up-and-coming business success.

With the help of a rather large mortgage from one of Jack's banker friends, the home was soon theirs. The memorandum title went into a file folder next to the file for the small apartment building that Jack and Diane owned, purchased with her salary from the OB/GYN office. Soon Diane was spending evenings and weekends shopping for furniture to fill their new home while Jack seemed to spend every waking hour at the new offices the friends had opened.

When they first married, all of this was a dream for the future. Now it was starting to happen, and it was time for their estate plan, first conceived after their prenuptial agreement, to catch up.

On Your Way Up and Accumulating Assets

Many people will encounter a time in their lives when they begin accumulating assets. Houses. Vacation homes. Stocks and bonds. Retirement plans. Business interests. Insurance. Tangible (physical) and intangible (non-physical) assets alike. This is a time to pay particular attention to how your estate is structured. Keeping everything in order, and maintaining a vision of how you want assets divided and distributed in the case of future marital problems or untimely deaths will help you weather any future storms with as little turbulence as possible.

If you don't keep things in order, chaos can ensue. Consider the situation where a man divorced and remarried without bothering to change the beneficiary designation on his life insurance policy. When he unexpectedly developed a ravenous form of cancer and died, his ex-wife and son received all the money from his policy although it was not required under the divorce decree. The simple lesson is that beneficiary designations trump what is said in a divorce decree or estate plan. A family's entire estate plan can be upended by poor follow-through or inattention to detail.

— *Basic ownership definitions* —

How you set up ownership of your growing assets determines the size of your estate, how it will pass and how easily it will pass. Understanding how assets can be owned is important when setting up a good estate plan. There are a few different ways joint or co-ownership relationships can be legally set up. Each has some plusses and minuses, depending on your specific estate planning needs.

Tenancy in common. This is a form of co-ownership. Tenancy in common allows multiple owners to leave their share of an asset to their designated heirs. Under tenancy in common, each owner can own different percentages. Two may own 25% while the third owns the remaining 50%. Ownership can also be obtained at different times, enabling new partners to join years after the initial ownership was gained.

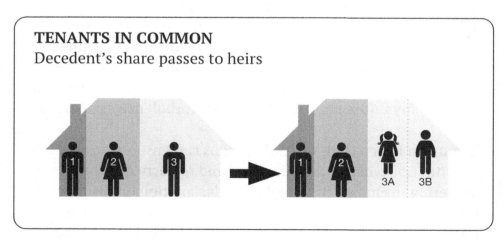

TENANTS IN COMMON
Decedent's share passes to heirs

For estate-planning purposes, tenancy in common owners have no survivorship rights. If one partner dies, their shares belong to the estate and are distributed according to will or trust designations.

Joint tenancy or joint tenants with rights of survivorship. This too is a form of joint ownership. Joint tenancy makes each person within the ownership group heirs to the other(s). Unlike tenancy in common, joint tenancy automatically transfers assets upon the death of each partner without involving probate. Joint tenants own equal shares that can be sold, gifted or passed on as part of their own estate. However, if one dies, their shares are absorbed by the other members of the ownership group. If there are three people in the ownership group, each owning one-third of the asset and one dies, the remaining owners will each own one-half.

JOINT TENANTS WITH RIGHTS OF SURVIVORSHIP
Decedents share passes to surviving owners

Joint tenants can sell their shares, but if they do, the ownership arrangement converts to tenancy in common. Joint tenancy arrangements can also be broken if one or more partners buy out the others or if surviving heirs file a partition action allowing them to sell their stake.

There are some disadvantages to joint tenancy, especially if the relationship between partners is unstable. Consider the dilemma Jack and Diane could find themselves in if they own an apartment building as tenants in common with one of Jack's business partners. If Jack and Diane's marriage, or the relationship between Jack and his business partner crumbled, none of the partners could sell their stake without the approval of the others.

Or, consider the situation if Jack and Diane own a commercial property as joint tenants and Jack dies first. Diane now owns the entire property and can do with it what she wants. She may well end up passing it on to a beneficiary. Jack would not want a shady second husband who Diane married on the rebound profiting from his hard work. In this case, Jack lost his ability to control who benefits from a key asset.

Default ownership arrangements. It should be noted that joint tenancy is the default ownership arrangement for married couples in some states, while tenancy in common or tenants by the entirety is the default arrangement in other states.

Tenants by the entirety. Another form of joint ownership, tenants by the entirety can only be held by married couples. Each partner owns the entirety of the asset rather than shares. This provides additional asset protection since the property cannot be targeted by creditors of one spouse or the other. The property is only exposed to creditors when both spouses are liable for the debt. One spouse also cannot mortgage, sell or otherwise encumber the property without consent from the other. Where other forms of ownership allow partners to sell or gift their shares, tenants by the entirety cannot sell an interest in the property since both spouses own 100%.

If a property is titled as tenants by the entirety and one spouse dies, the surviving spouse becomes the sole owner. If there is a divorce, depending on its terms, tenancy by the entirety is dissolved and the property can be re-titled as a sole ownership, joint tenancy or tenancy in common.

TENANTS BY THE ENTIRETY
Spouses own 100% of asset as fused marital unit

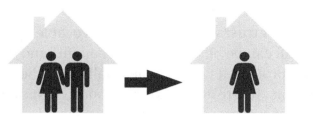

Tenants by the entirety is currently recognized in about half of all states. To see if your state allows this ownership arrangement, see Chapter 16.

The rules for tenants in the entirety vary by state and can be used on any property in most states where it is an option. However, in Illinois, this form of ownership is only available to couples for their homestead, not investment real estate.

The rules of your state will, therefore, play a large role in how your accumulated property is titled. Consider, for instance, if Jack and Diane lived in Illinois and held title to the new Glencoe house as tenants in the entirety. If Jack died, the title to the property would automatically pass to Diane outright and free of trust. She would then own the home entirely in her name (and would have to transfer the property to her living trust to avoid probate). A creditor would find the home an attractive asset to go after.

However, Illinois allows couples to hold title to their primary residence through their trusts as tenants in the entirety. This form of ownership provides the best estate planning and asset protection benefits. During their lifetimes, the property would be owned by them through their trusts as a fused marital unit and remain asset protected from their individual creditors. Upon Jack's death, the tenants by the entirety ownership is severed and each of their trusts would own half the house. Jack's trust would become irrevocable upon his death (but still can be held for Diane's benefit) and would remain asset protected while Diane's half would be reachable by her creditors. Interestingly, since Diane's trust only owns a partial piece of real estate, the property is far less attractive to creditors.

Funding Trusts

If you have trusts in place, be diligent in making sure you properly fund your trusts and update beneficiary designations to ensure you and your loved ones can reap the benefits of this wonderful estate planning tool.

Unless married couples live in a community property state, each spouse should have a separate revocable living trust to leverage tax planning and provide asset protection for their beneficiaries. In a traditional revocable living trust, you are the grantor or settlor of the trust and you are the sole trustee of the trust during your lifetime (or a co-trustee with a spouse). Thus, you have full authority over the trust assets. Because you are the grantor and trustee, no separate tax identification number or annual maintenance is required.

People often ask, "Doesn't my pour-over will automatically ensure the assets avoid probate?" The pour-over will ensures that assets left in your individual name and without beneficiary designations will be distributed through your revocable living trust. Unfortunately, if the cumulative value of assets in your individual name exceeds the probate threshold, they will first have to go through probate and then pour over into your trust. The threshold to avoid probate varies dramatically from state to state ($100,000 in Illinois, $75,000 in Florida and only $30,000 in New York). See the chart on Chapter 16 for a summary of the threshold to avoid probate in various states. As we saw earlier in this chapter, regardless of what the trust documents (or a divorce decree) may provide, the beneficiary designations on life insurance, retirement plan accounts and bank accounts govern. Thus, it is critical to retitle assets and update beneficiary designations.

If you live in the rare state that allows married couples to hold virtually any asset (bank accounts, real estate and business interests) as tenants by the entirety, you can leverage asset protection from ownership without fully funding your revocable living trust.

For married couples who previously relied on joint titling as a tool to avoid probate, the majority of assets previously held jointly should be separated and divided equally into two separate trust accounts. Or, if the financial institution allows it, hold title through your two trusts, as tenants in common, which means that each of your trusts owns a 50% interest in the account.

Retitling Assets

Here's a quick look at how to retitle assets consistent with your estate planning needs.

For married couples with separate trusts: If in addition to your separate trusts, you wish to also hold title to assets together, you can inquire with your bank or investment firm as to whether they allow an account to be held by both trusts, as tenants in common (half considered owned by each trust). Alternatively, couples can put different assets in different trusts in an attempt to equalize taxable gross estates. Although portability at the federal level makes this less of an issue, couples are often encouraged to have roughly an equivalent value in one another's estates in an effort to leverage estate tax planning. For example, if one spouse has a large life insurance policy or large retirement plan, maybe the savings account will be placed in the other spouse's trust. Regardless of how things are set up today, if you later look back and realize that one spouse's trust has significantly more assets, it is easy to move assets between the trusts without any income tax or gift tax implications.

Another question that often arises for married couples is what happens in the event of a divorce with certain assets in one living trust or the other? Any marital assets will still be deemed marital assets regardless of whose trust they are in. The marital separation agreement would then provide for how assets should be transferred or divided.

Any marital assets will still be deemed marital assets regardless of whose trust they are in

Checking accounts. Checking accounts with small balances may be kept in your individual name or may be held as joint tenants with rights of survivorship if you are married. If you elect to keep a checking account in your individual name or titled jointly, be sure to monitor the balance. And consider naming adult children as the beneficiaries through a "transfer on death" or "payable on death" designation on the account. If the bank allows, you may also consider naming your trust as the "transfer on death" or "payable on death" designation.

Alternatively, your trust may maintain its own checking account, which should be registered with your bank in the name of your trust. Each bank has its own procedure, but a letter of direction or new account application is usually enough to change ownership.

Savings accounts and certificates of deposit. Ownership of your savings accounts and certificates of deposit can be transferred to your trust by filling out a form available from your financial institution. These accounts and certificates should also be registered in the name of your trust. Be sure the institution does not treat this change as a withdrawal causing you to lose interest. Point out that the funds are not being withdrawn from the bank and the only change is the name on the account.

Stocks and bonds. Stocks, bonds and mutual fund shares may be added to your trust by transferring ownership through a transfer agent. Your broker should be able to assist you in this matter. If you do not have a broker, it will be necessary to call the transfer agent and request the documents necessary to make the transfer. This also holds true for any paper stocks or bonds you may have. For many people this is an opportune time to consider consolidation of assets. The hassle now pales in comparison to what your family will have to go through in the probate process.

Interests in real estate. If you own real estate in multiple states in your individual name, you run the risk of having to open a probate estate in each of those states. Therefore, it is critical that you retitle real estate interests to avoid probate.

Single people should transfer ownership of all real estate holdings to their trust. Whereas, in the few states allowing real estate to be held by trusts as tenants by the entirety, married couples should title their primary residence to their revocable living trusts as tenants by the entirety. Under tenants by the entirety, only a joint creditor of both spouses may reach the underlying real estate, but a creditor of either spouse cannot. For real estate located in other states, it is important to consult with your attorney. The ownership nuances vary dramatically from state to state. Florida, Michigan and New Jersey, for example, allow for any real property to be held as tenants by the entirety. Therefore, in some instances, people may elect to keep real estate held as tenants by the entirety for the asset protection benefits and retitle real estate into trusts in the future when asset protection concerns subside. And if real estate holdings include rental properties, consider a limited liability company to hold title to the property to help insulate you from liability.

Business entities. Wherever possible, ownership in any corporations, partnerships or limited liability companies should be in the name of your trust. Sometimes, the organizational documents for the business entity may limit transfers of ownership but, even in those instances, they will often explicitly authorize a transfer to a revocable living trust.

Safe deposit boxes. Ownership of safe deposit boxes can be shifted to the trust by execution of the appropriate forms provided by the safe deposit box company.

IRA's and qualified plans. For married couples who do not have children from a prior marriage, the initial beneficiary of these plans should be your spouse. In this manner, the surviving spouse may roll over the inherited IRA into his or her own through a "spousal rollover," allowing for maximum deferral of income tax liabilities and continued asset protection. Unfortunately, the same is not true for other beneficiaries.

In 2014, the U.S. Supreme Court held that inherited, non-spousal IRAs can be claimed by creditors in bankruptcy proceedings. For this reason, you should consider naming your trust as the contingent beneficiary. People with minor children or beneficiaries with creditor concerns (or the potential for creditors) should list a trust as a beneficiary.

In the past, an inherited IRA that passed to someone other than a spouse could be stretched over the beneficiary's life expectancy. But as of January 1, 2020, the Setting Every Community Up for Retirement Enhancements (the "SECURE") Act dramatically limited the ability to stretch an inherited IRA. Under the SECURE Act, unless a beneficiary is an "eligible designated beneficiary," the beneficiary must withdraw the IRA within 10 years. Eligible designated beneficiaries include the following:
- Surviving spouse
- Minor child
- Disabled / chronically ill person
- Person who is not more than 10 years younger than the decedent

If the retirement plans are modest and there are not creditor concerns, individual beneficiaries can be listed. However, if there are creditor concerns or if you wish to control the flow of funds (make the trust available for one beneficiary and then pass to a subsequent), your trust should be listed as a primary or contingent beneficiary.

A number of years ago the IRS took the stand that if a trust is the beneficiary of a retirement plan, it is impossible to know how old the trust is. This made the trust an unidentifiable beneficiary that would have to be cashed out within five years of the grantor's death. However, if your trust includes specific "stretch IRA" or "conduit trust" language, the plan administrator can look through the trust to the life expectancy of the beneficiaries in determining the required minimum distributions. Absent such language, the trust may not be an identifiable beneficiary and the IRA may need to be cashed out within five years of the owner's death with devastating tax consequences.

Single clients may list a trust as the primary beneficiary by delivering a change of beneficiary form to the plan's trustee or sponsor.

If you have charitable intentions, you may allocate a percentage of your traditional IRA to a charitable organization or group of organizations. By making charitable bequests directly from an IRA, the proceeds are both estate and income tax free, which can translate into tax savings exceeding 70% when you combine the federal and state income and estate tax implications. Read more about charitable planning opportunities in Chapter 12.

By making charitable bequests directly from an IRA, the proceeds are both estate and income tax free

---

Life insurance policies. Life insurance policies have beneficiary designations so they automatically avoid probate. However, trusts are still critical to ensure that the proceeds will be 1) asset protected for beneficiaries, 2) pass in the most tax efficient manner, and 3) avoid guardian estates for minor children. Your trust should be the beneficiary of all life insurance, and your insurance agent, or the company itself, can provide change of beneficiary forms.

Depending on the amount of insurance you have and the size of your overall estate, it may be beneficial to create an irrevocable life insurance trust (ILIT) to be the owner and beneficiary to ensure proceeds pass estate tax free. Be sure to consult with your attorney if your life insurance is required to be maintained by a divorce decree or buy-sell agreement in connection with business interests. Learn more about how and when to layer in an ILIT in Chapter 8.

Personal property. Many revocable living trusts incorporate a transfer of personal property as part of a schedule to the trust covering jewelry, artwork, automobiles and boats. If your trust does not include this, you may wish to have a separate grant and assignment of personal property, which is generally a one-page document assigning all personal property to your trust.

Setting Up Powers of Attorney

As you accumulate assets, you may find yourselves in need of updated powers of attorney appointing someone to act on your behalf if you are not available or become incapacitated. This can be done by filling out a simple form available online or prepared by your attorney. In most states, in order to be valid, they must be notarized and witnessed.

Powers of attorney (POA) are governed by state law, so be sure any forms you sign conform to the laws of your state. POAs can be either limited or general depending on your needs. Also, consider getting healthcare POAs for any adult children. Just because you are paying college tuition for a child does not mean that you would have access to their medical information in the event of an emergency.

Limited power of attorney. Limited POAs are executed for a specific purpose. Perhaps you need to be out of town on the day a real estate transfer is to take place. A limited power of attorney will allow your real estate agent or another person to complete the sale in your absence.

General power of attorney. A general POA enables someone else to act on your behalf with all the rights and powers you have yourself. For example, a general power of attorney allows someone to sign documents, pay debts, purchase assets and conduct financial transactions in your stead and on your behalf. And, if you have a revocable living trust, make sure your power of attorney authorizes your agent to transfer assets from your name into your trust. I often discover people have assets in their names after they have lost their ability to manage their own affairs. By allowing your agent to have this power, the designated agent can help transfer assets to your trust to avoid probate issues for your family in the future.

Keep Your Advisors on the Same Page

As you start to accumulate assets, your estate planning goals may change. Your total assets may start hovering near exemption levels you previously thought unattainable. You may find yourselves needing more liquidity than before. Just as likely, you may suddenly find that you need to do a better job of protecting assets and planning for sophisticated distributions in the event of one spouse dying at an early age. In these cases, it is important to update your plan to keep pace with new realities.

Just as important is to make sure all your legal and financial advisors are on the same page. Your professional fees are wasted if your CPA is unaware of changes you made to your estate plan that would necessitate the retitling of certain assets.

Conversation Starters
Building Wealth

As assets begin to accumulate, conversations should start involving asset protection as well as future beneficiaries. It is easy to let things slide as wealth grows and more demands are placed on your time. However, mistakes at this stage of your life can have far-reaching consequences.

1. **As we start accumulating these new things, would it be a good idea to bring outside partners into the mix?**
   Risk and reward are always important as you start investing in more property and intangible assets. However, you need to consider the kind of ownership structure you and your partners will have. Talk about the importance of being able to sell your stakes and the possibility of a crumbling relationship, especially with business partners.

2. **Do you see us buying and selling property on a regular basis, or should we be keeping everything as a long-term investment?**
   Certain types of ownership are more conducive to frequent sales. Your goal may be to hold properties long term, building an estate for your heirs. Do you envision renting the property out? If so, is there sufficient property and casualty insurance — and should you consider a limited liability company to protect your other assets from the reach of a tenant?

3. **There's going to be a lot of work involved in acquiring the kind of property we've been talking about. Whom do we want to inherit it if something happens to one of us?**

   Look out for unintended consequences. Under joint tenancy ownership, an asset may well end up with someone you don't want to benefit from your hard work.

4. **Do we know the default ownership arrangements in our state?**

   A good place to start any titling conversation is with the default position. Knowing the laws in your state will greatly influence future decisions.

5. **Did we envision owning these types of assets when we first set up our estate plan?**

   It is hard to see the future and it is very likely your current estate plan doesn't fit with your new circumstances. You may never know when your life will end, but you can always be prepared. A good estate plan will grow with you.

6. **What would happen to our property and other assets if we were both to die in a car crash?**

   Most default ownership arrangements are set up to deal with assets moving to a survivor. However, are you and your spouse prepared if both of you were to die at the same time? Without proper preparation, the bulk of your estate could easily end up in a lengthy probate — or guardian estates if assets pass to minor children without a proper plan.

7. **When it comes to investment properties, how much control do we need to have?**

   Depending on how your assets are titled, you can have

greater or less control of them both during your lifetime and after. Before the initial purchase, you must make ownership decisions that account for contingencies that ensure your wishes are met.

8. **How close are we to estate tax exemption levels?**
As your circumstances change, your estate planning needs will become more complex. Knowing where you stand in terms of both state and federal exemption levels is critical to your changing estate planning needs. It is also important to remember that the exemption levels change periodically and what was true five years ago may not be true today.

Chapter 8
Jack and Diane Start a Family

The world was spinning when Diane left work one hot July evening. Years later she would remember everything about that evening. The smell of poppies in the flower pots by the entrance to the OB/GYN clinic where she worked. The feel of the leather steering wheel on her new Audi. The concerned look the older couple had given her when they passed on the sidewalk. It was one of those monumental days ingrained in her brain for eternity.

She'd been feeling a bit drained for two weeks and her stomach always seemed a bit queasy. Uncharacteristically, she'd had a hard time getting out of bed in the morning. Jack was preoccupied with a new business deal, so she had not yet mentioned anything to him. But she knew.

They had never really discussed starting a family. Both had always said they wanted children... sometime. However, they had never actually decided when that time might be. Somehow, they both thought it would just happen. Now it had.

Earlier that morning Diane had mentioned her symptoms and suspicions to Dr. Julie Drendel, her favorite doctor in the practice. Julie agreed to run a test and later pulled Diane into her office with a big smile on her face.

After hearing that she was indeed pregnant, Diane felt the room start to spin just a bit. Enough to make her a bit disconcerted as she looked for a phone to call Jack. Jack's assistant answered his phone and told Diane that Jack was stuck in a meeting but would call her as soon as he was done. In the meantime, her emotions remained pent up.

When they finally connected, Jack sounded happy but, perhaps, a bit anxious. He told Diane he'd come home as soon as possible so they could talk. Three hours later he finally walked through the front door.

Two weeks later, after both Jack and Diane had a chance to adjust to the news, they shared a special celebratory dinner and simply talked. They decided they needed to make an appointment with their estate planning attorney because their lives were about to change dramatically.

The Importance of Children in Estate Planning

In many ways Jack and Diane are unique in the fact that they kept on top of their estate planning needs from the moment they decided to marry. Many people need a stronger push to start putting their estate planning into high gear. Most often children are that impetus.

No matter when you start or update your estate plan, there will be major changes when children come along. Most changes relate to the need to update beneficiaries. You will also want to make sure your estate plan provides security for your children before they reach the age of maturity, protection until they reach actual maturity and an inheritance when you are gone. Many expecting parents are thrilled to learn that future children can automatically be provided for. In this way, couples can get their estate planning in place prior to the arrival of their little bundles of joy.

— *New children. New responsibilities.* —————

When children come along, it is a joyous time. Unfortunately, you need to also think about the unthinkable. What happens if you and your spouse are no longer in the picture.

There are two ways guardianships can be formed for minor children. The least preferable of your options is to have a judge, who knows little about you and your family, appoint a guardian. The best option is for you to plan for any eventuality and take control of your children's future, whether you're there or not.

Appointing guardians. First of all, you may want to appoint two different guardians:

- One to manage the guardian estate and make sure your children's financial needs are taken care of
- Another to care for their social, educational and emotional needs

In an ideal world, your estate plan incorporates revocable living trusts and a majority of the assets would pass to children through a trust and not through a guardian estate. If a guardian of the estate is required, separate guardian estates are necessary for each minor child, and the guardian would be required to report to the court annually regarding the disposition of the estate. With guardian estates, once children reach the age of 18, they have complete access to all of the funds.

Assets passing to children through trust do not require guardian estates and can, therefore, provide additional protective mechanisms to further delay the age at which the children have complete access. A family member or friend could look after the funds as trustee of the children's trust and determine when distributions should be made for a child. Then, when the child reaches a certain age, perhaps 30, they can start acting as their own trustee.

Even when trusts are in place, guardian estates are still necessary to cover any uniform transfer to minors' accounts, etc. At the end of the day the guardian of the estate would be whomever you trust to make financial or administrative decisions on behalf of the children. It could also be a corporate bank or other fiduciary assigned to look after the funds.

Even when trusts are in place, guardian estates are still necessary

Guardian of the person would be an individual or couple you trust to look after and raise the children. Both sets of guardians should be individuals who share your values and understand your dreams for your children's future. Parents often inquire whether the person who looks after the funds should also look after the children — or if different individuals should be appointed. The decision varies for each family. For some, the idea of a check and balance is important — for others, you may trust your sister, Emily, to look after the children and manage the funds. At the end of the day, listen to your gut instinct regarding who is best suited to act. If it is the same person, that's fine...and if they are different individuals, that can work as well.

When someone dies with minor children, and has named different guardians to look after the money versus raise the children, the attorney will typically facilitate a meeting for them to set up some type of budget to handle everyday expenses.

As the children grow, the budget would be revised to alleviate the administrative stress associated with reimbursement for everyday necessities for the children and allows guardians to focus on caring for the kids.

The need for successor guardians. What happens when something happens to the people you initially appoint as guardians? It would not be unusual for a guardian to face their own health, emotional or financial challenges. You may also find that people say yes when initially asked to serve as guardians, but circumstances change by the time a guardian is needed. For this reason, it is always a good idea for you to appoint successor guardians.

A grandmother and grandfather may be fine if they are under the age of 65, but consider trusted in-laws, siblings, extended family and friends, too. Others you would trust with the future of your children can be named successor guardians.

Guardians are appointed in will documents so it is important to make sure they remain up to date. If there are changes to make in guardianship arrangements, they must be done with a codicil, or a modification to the original will.

Making your desires known. Appointing guardians is an emotional decision. The ones you appoint will guide your children's futures. For this reason, consider writing a letter expressing your dreams and desires for them, though the letters are not legally binding, they provide a way for you to maintain some influence on decisions guardians make.

— New children. New beneficiaries. —

Children change everything. Families with children are families with a longer future. Suddenly there is a next generation to consider. In addition to a surviving spouse, you now have direct heirs, which provides opportunity as well as responsibility.

With the addition of a new generation, there is now the potential to carry wealth forward and a renewed reason to protect assets. The first step is updating beneficiary designations on wills and trusts and confirming the titling of assets and beneficiary designations on life insurance and retirement plans to ensure that they comport with your overall estate plan. Obviously, if these are not already in place, now is a good time to get moving and have these basic estate planning tools developed.

Planning for Their Future with 529 Plans

In many ways your children's future depends on the things you do now. Parents who care enough about the future to do estate planning certainly want the best for their children, and that is the time to put thoughts into action.

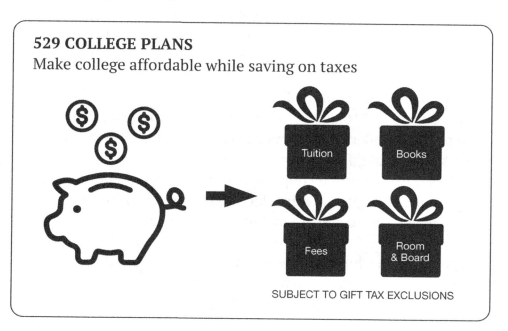

529 COLLEGE PLANS
Make college affordable while saving on taxes

Tuition

Books

Fees

Room & Board

SUBJECT TO GIFT TAX EXCLUSIONS

Today, any successful future requires some form of higher education. Many parents are also concerned about the rising cost of private K-12 schools. With education costs rising faster than inflation, it is never too early to start planning for how you'll handle those future expenses.

Any family with future educational aspirations should consider 529 college savings plans. These government sponsored plans allow you to save tax-free money for future educational expenses. The money put into these savings accounts can also be withdrawn tax free with one big caveat: they can only be used for educational expenses, including tuition, books, fees and room and board.

If the money in 529 college savings plans is used for any expense other than education, state and federal income taxes will be owed with an additional 10% penalty. Interestingly, if your child turns out to be remarkably gifted and earns a full scholarship, an amount equal to the scholarship can be withdrawn without penalty (but income taxes will still apply). It always pays to have a child who is smart, athletic or both.

Contributions to a 529 college savings plan are considered gifts and, subsequently, qualify for the federal gift tax exclusion, currently up to $16,000 per year (or $32,000 for a married couple). The federal government also allows for gifting of five years of annual gifts at once. Lump sum gifts up to $80,000 (or $160,000 for a married couple) are not considered part of your federal lifetime gifts and, by electing the five-year exclusion, you can get a head start in making a lump sum contribution.

Depending on where you reside, some states offer additional benefits for residents who make 529 plan contributions. For example, the BrightStart plan in Illinois offers a state level income tax deduction on the first $10,000 contribution made by an individual (or $20,000 for a couple). This enables taxpayers to save tax-free money while gaining an additional state tax deduction if the contribution is made before filing your return. Oregon offers a similar plan with a deduction limit of $2,435 per person and $4,865 for a couple filing jointly. Visit *www. savingforcollege.com* for specific comparisons of state plans.

For this reason, be strategic in the timing of your contributions. David and Jamie received an inheritance from David's grandmother and expressed an interest in making a $30,000 contribution in a single year and then skipping the next year. As residents of Illinois, they had to consider the state level income tax deductions. For them, it actually made more sense to contribute $20,000 in the current year and $10,000 in the next to take advantage of the state level income tax deductions.

And, for those families with a special needs child, the government has created ABLE accounts to provide similar benefits.

— *Larger gifting for children* —

Often, funding education and college expenses is a primary concern for parents when it comes to providing for their children. Once education plans are taken care of, parents in a position to continue gifting on a regular basis can by creating a trust for their children. If the children are young, often times a single trust for the benefit of multiple children is a nice way to streamline administration. Separate trusts for each child can also be created. However, for many families, greater financial freedom comes later in life — once children are already grown and the focus extends beyond children to grandchildren. A more in-depth discussion of gift trusts for children (or grandchildren) and other strategies for generous parents and grandparents can be found in Chapter 9.

— *Provide financial security for your family with insurance* —

The time when children arrive is also a good time to review your insurance program because the problem with life is...you never know what tomorrow may bring. If something happens to you, how will their financial needs be covered? Insurance is purchased to provide financial support to someone else, in this case, your surviving spouse and children.

In today's modern world there are different considerations than previous generations faced. Today, Jack may well be the one who decides to stay home and care for the children. What if something happens to Diane? How will Jack cover basic expenses? When planning your insurance policies, you will probably want to consider how your children's lives will continue if the breadwinner dies. Insurance can be used to cover future college expenses, pay off mortgages, pay off other large financial obligations, and to cover expenses as your family grieves and transitions.

Also, people often insure only the breadwinner in the family but forget to consider what happens if the nurturing spouse dies. How will childcare expenses be covered? As a society, we have difficulty putting a financial value on the contributions of a nurturing spouse, however, the costs become real if something happens to them.

In many cases you may find the need to fill financial holes with insurance policies primed to provide tax-free money to secure your children's future. Remember, the death benefit of any life insurance is what is included in your taxable gross estate. For many couples, the insurance death benefit makes their estates taxable. For others, there may be sufficient funds to provide for one another, but it is evident that there will be an estate tax liability. In those instances, couples sometimes shift their focus to life insurance to act as an estate tax replacement vehicle.

This may be a good time to set up an irrevocable life insurance trust (ILIT). This kind of trust can hold multiple insurance policies and use the proceeds to cover estate taxes, income taxes and other immediate needs. But, by making the ILIT the owner and beneficiary of the policy, the death benefit can pass estate tax free to beneficiaries.

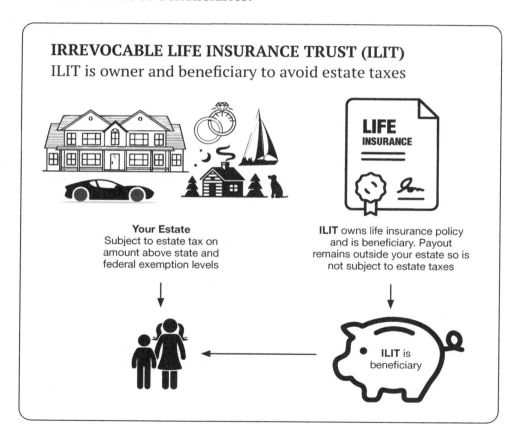

IRREVOCABLE LIFE INSURANCE TRUST (ILIT)
ILIT is owner and beneficiary to avoid estate taxes

Your Estate
Subject to estate tax on amount above state and federal exemption levels

ILIT owns life insurance policy and is beneficiary. Payout remains outside your estate so is not subject to estate taxes

ILIT is beneficiary

When a new life insurance policy will be owned by the ILIT, you will need the trustee to sign the application for the new policy.

You, as the insured, will need to qualify for the policy. Be sure the ILIT is already in existence when the policy is issued. If the policy is already owned by you, you can subsequently transfer the policy to the ILIT, but there are gift considerations you need to discuss with your insurance broker and estate attorney.

To fund an ILIT with existing policies, you'll need to take a number of administrative steps:

1. The ILIT will need an employer identification number (EIN), which is typically obtained by the estate planning attorney.

2. You will need to complete two forms from the issuing insurance company. The trustee of the ILIT will have to sign both forms
   - Change of owner/assignment form
   - Change of beneficiary form

3. You will need to submit all forms to the insurance company. **Remember to confirm that the insurance company has made the necessary changes.**

4. The trustee will have to open a bank account in the name of the ILIT. Since the ILIT now owns the insurance policies, the trustee will have to make all premium payments using monies you gift to the trust.

5. Send "Crummey Notices," which are simply letters, to beneficiaries as described below. And, depending on the laws in your state, sometimes a general notice to beneficiaries of the irrevocable trust is also required.

On an annual basis when premiums are due, the insured would transfer funds to the ILIT account and the trustee of the ILIT would then transmit the funds to the insurance provider. When the premium payments are made, they are considered deemed gifts to the beneficiaries (often a spouse and children). In order for the premiums to be considered annual exclusion gifts, the IRS requires the beneficiary to have a "present interest" in the gift. Therefore, each year the trustee must send each beneficiary a "Crummey Notice" notifying the beneficiary that a contribution was made to the trust and the beneficiary has a right to withdraw the funds. The amount, which is considered an annual exclusion gift, needs to be taken into consideration when you are planning to make other annual gifts to a 529 plan or children's trust(s). To the extent the premiums exceed the annual exclusion amount for a beneficiary, a gift tax form must be filed. Recall, typically no gift tax is owed, but the IRS requires an informational return.

As your estate grows over time, it may also make sense to look at a second-to-die life insurance policy to act as an estate tax replacement vehicle. Specifically, many clients invest in life insurance to help cover the forecasted estate tax liabilities. With the collaboration of the financial planner (running projections on your future net worth and spending habits), the insurance broker, and the estate planning attorney, your advisory team can help create a plan to meet your personal needs. For married couples in good health, a second-to-die insurance policy is often a wonderful planning tool because it pays out upon the death of both parties and is often less expensive than a single life policy. Assuming you have a properly structured estate plan to ensure that no estate tax is owed until both spouses have passed away, the timing of the insurance payout mirrors the timing of the estate tax liability. In addition to the estate tax planning benefits, death benefits on life insurance are also income tax free.

Remember, an irrevocable trust removes assets from your control. While small administrative changes can be made, the beneficiaries or flow of funds cannot be amended or changed once it has been executed.

After you have explored funding 529 plans and insurance, to the extent you are in a financial position, consider making additional gifts to your children's trusts. These concepts are explored more in Chapter 9 when we look at planning tools for generous grandparents.

— *Maximizing your children's inheritance* —

In most cases this means minimizing the bite taxes can take from your estate. However, it may also mean protecting assets from creditors. In both cases good estate planning is a necessity. A substantial portion of your children's inheritance could easily be lost to court actions simply because some basic estate planning concepts were overlooked.

Conversation Starters
Family Time

As noted above, children change everything. As a couple, or even as a single parent, you've likely had many conversations related to child-rearing. You've probably talked about how to raise children to become good, successful people. Take some time to also have conversations about how to finance their young lives and how to both maximize and protect their inheritance.

1. **What happens if, God forbid, something happens to one of us and that person can no longer contribute to support our children?**

This is one of two key questions to ask when children come along. It should lead you into a discussion of insurance options that can supplement the income if one spouse dies or help support the family until the surviving spouse figures out how to make ends meet.

2. **How much do you think college will cost by the time our child graduates high school? How will we pay for it?**
    This is the other key question. How will you afford a good future for your children? Education is probably the most important and potentially expensive parts of this equation. Thinking about college when your children are born, or even before, is a large step forward in finding an affordable solution.

3. **Until now we've both been working. Will one of us now stay home to be with our child? If you become the nurturing parent, how will we afford to take care of all the things you do if something happens to you?**
    It is too easy to overlook the value the nurturing spouse brings to family finances. Daycare, cleaning, laundry services and more all cost money if the nurturing spouse is no longer in the picture. Keep this in mind as you develop your estate plan.

4. **Out of all the people we know, who would be best suited to care for our kids if something happened to us? Who would we trust if something happened to the original guardians? Should we appoint separate financial guardians?**
    Perhaps the most important decision you'll make as a parent is who to trust if you're no longer around. Things

happen even to the best people, but by choosing guardians and successor guardians, you'll help ensure your children's lives move forward after catastrophe.

5. **Should we be making beneficiary changes to our retirement, insurance and trust accounts? How can we pass these assets to our children without paying big taxes?**
At the heart of any good estate plan is both the smooth delivery of assets to the intended beneficiaries and the minimization of taxes owed on property passed from one generation to the next.

6. **How are our assets owned and titled? What happens if we die and some creditor decides to sue our estate? Are we sure our children's inheritance is protected?**
Asset protection is as important as tax minimization. Now is the time to consider how you can protect your assets in order to make sure your children inherit maximum value.

Chapter 9
Grandchildren Come Along

One fall morning Diane was home with her youngest daughter Katie; the only child still at home. The older children, Whitney and Ethan, had flown the nest, leaving Katie alone with Diane.

Jack was rarely home with his impressive business demanding most of his time. The small investment firm he'd started with three friends had grown faster and further than they originally thought it would, though not yet as far as they'd dreamed.

While Diane sat at the kitchen table drinking coffee next to Katie, whose nose was in her phone, she looked out at the beautifully trimmed hedges leading down to the stables behind their Fox Valley home. This is the house her children call home. It is where they'd spent their most formative years. Where Whitney learned to ride, where Ethan spent hours reading books about other cultures and places, and where Katie's graduation party will be held. Whitney was married in the back yard and the kids' friends still stopped by to say hello.

Whitney is a journalist in New York and Ethan is in law school in Washington, D.C., studying to become an environmental attorney. Diane missed them both dearly. Since she stopped working at the OB/GYN clinic, the children had been her life. Now, with Katie in her senior year, Diane's world seemed to be narrowing.

As George Harrison's song "Here Comes the Sun" rang from her cell phone, Diane knew it was Whitney. It was the song she'd sung to her as a child and it fit her personality perfectly. She picked it up to hear her oldest daughter laughing and crying on the other end of the line.

"Mom ... you're going to be a grandmother!!"

The words sent a joyful tremor through Diane's body. She was at once thrilled and scared, just like she'd been when she found out she was pregnant with Whitney those many years ago. Had it really been 26 years? Why had time moved so fast?

Whitney was beyond ecstatic, and Diane shared her enthusiasm. But, the word "grandmother" sat a bit heavily on her shoulders. She wasn't quite sure how she felt about being someone's grandmother. However, she was sure about one thing as she picked up the phone to give Jack the news. It was time to call their estate planning attorney, again.

New Estate Planning Challenges and Opportunities

As families grow, adding generations, your list of potential beneficiaries also grows. This new generation not only adds to your responsibilities, but also expands your ability to minimize estate taxes and pass along more of a large estate tax free. As mentioned in Chapter 8, all of the strategies outlined here are applicable to both children and grandchildren.

Another generation to care for and educate. If you thought college and private education costs were high when you sent your children to school, wait until you see how they balloon in the future. College tuition has been rising at approximately 6% per year according to the College Board and the investment management company Vanguard. That means children born in 2022 will face upper education costs of $120,000 per year at private schools and $54,000 per year at public institutions. The cost of your grandchildren's college education could easily surpass a quarter to half a million dollars, making it harder for your grandchildren to assume college loan debt. Thus, grandparents with means can pass a larger part of their estate tax free to future generations.

As we discussed in Chapter 7, 529 college savings plans are a tax-advantaged investment vehicle designed to encourage saving for educational expenses of a designated beneficiary, including grandchildren. These plans are considered taxable gifts, so they provide another means of gifting to a third generation. In 2022, donors can contribute up to $80,000 per year for each beneficiary or $160,000 for a married couple, prorated over five years, without incurring a federal gift tax. However, an informational gift tax return must be filed.

At the same time, capital appreciation in assets used to fund these accounts are tax deferred. Many states also provide income tax deductions for contributions to these plans. In Illinois, individuals making contributions can deduct a maximum of up to $10,000 or $20,000 per couple on their state income taxes. For this reason, when my nieces and nephews, who live in New York and Massachusetts, joined our family, I encouraged my parents to open 529 plans in their resident state of Illinois. As Illinois residents, they could contribute up to $30,000 per grandchild annually. However, the state allowed for a state level income tax deduction on the first $20,000 annually.

As we discussed in Chapter 7, all appreciation of 529 plan investments are income tax free and distributions from these plans can be made for qualified educational expenses, including tuition, fees, books and most room and board. Distributions made for unrelated expenses are subject to income tax and penalties.

In addition, under Section 2503(e) of the Internal Revenue Code, tuition payments made directly to an educational organization (for anything from private nursery schools to graduate programs) are not considered gifts. In this way, generous grandparents can help subsidize education expenses for their grandchildren — and still make annual exclusion gifts.

With respect to educational expenses, the gift tax exclusion is only for tuition payments, not room, board or other ancillary expenses. In addition, the payments cannot be made to reimburse someone for the expenses; payments must be made directly to the institutional provider.

Providing Care for Another Generation

As grandchildren grow up, they may well experience illness and sudden medical expenses. Again, grandparents with means can be of great help by contributing directly to their medical expenses. Direct contributions to medical providers are tax free, however, you cannot reimburse a third party. The checks must be written directly to the medical facility.

For these families, the generous givers should consider getting credit cards for each family member. In this way, a family member receiving the benefits can simply charge a co-pay for a doctor's visit or medical expense to a credit card that would be paid for by the generous grandparent. Family credit cards used for education and medical payments help streamline the payment of expenses — and allows grandparents to accumulate more miles to visit their loved ones!

Generous Grandparents

My nieces, nephews and my own little guy bring immeasurable joy to our family, including their grandparents who are generous in everything they do. They, like countless other grandparents always say, "I want to see my children and grandchildren enjoy the fruits of our labors. What should we do?" The key is to gift strategically.

Gifting plays a critical role in transferring wealth from grandparents to grandchildren

As is true with parent to child wealth transfers where taxable gross estates are involved, gifting plays a critical role in transferring wealth from grandparents to grandchildren. Even for those with more modest means, it is important to incorporate strategic adjustments when gifting to new generations.

— *A new generation to gift* —

In the last chapter we discussed how gifts are powerful ways to pass estates from one generation to the next. Adding another generation increases your leverage. This is especially helpful for grandparents with estates larger than the federal exemption level looking for ways to minimize taxes while directing parts of their estates to different beneficiaries.

With the ability to currently gift up to $16,000 per person per year and up to $12.06 million throughout your lifetime, quite a bit of money or assets can be gifted to children and grandchildren. However, be careful if these grandchildren have special needs or run into severe medical problems. Once a gift is made to a beneficiary, it is considered part of their estate. If there's a situation where government services are needed, these gifts could possibly end up disqualifying them from access to needed programs.

Unfortunately, if a gift is not made in a particular calendar year, it cannot be rolled over to the next year. Use it or lose it.

For example, if grandma wanted to gift $116,000 to her grandson, $16,000 would be considered an annual gift and she would have to file a gift tax return notifying the IRS she has used $100,000 of her lifetime gift exemption. Upon her death she will be able to pass the lifetime exemption at the time (less the $100,000 she used during her lifetime). No gift tax would be owed, but the return must be filed for informational purposes.

— *Gifting to grandchildren without a trust or guardian*

The Uniform Gift to Minors Act (UGMA) was put in place to allow the transfer of securities to minor beneficiaries without going through a guardian or trustee. The subsequent Uniform Transfers to Minors Act (UTMA) extended this privilege to the transfer of money, patents, royalties, real estate and fine art.

For clients who envision making annual gifts over several years, the money can quickly grow. Once the money is in the UTMA or custodial account, it is considered the child's and cannot be put into a traditional gift trust. However, one option is to transfer the property to a 2503(c) trust which allows the assets to be held in trust for a minor beneficiary provided that they have a 30- to 60-day window to withdraw all of the principal and income upon turning 21.

Another option is to transfer the funds to a limited liability company managed by a parent. Keep in mind that once the funds are gifted to a minor outright, they are included in the minor's taxable gross estate. With proper planning, clients are encouraged to consider trusts instead of UTMAs for the estate tax and asset protection benefits.

There have been countless situations where the family has generously contributed to UTMA or custodial accounts only to later discover the child beneficiary has special needs. In those instances, it becomes a race against time to try and spend down those funds to ensure the child can qualify for benefits at the federal and state level. It is not necessarily a situation where the family wishes to take advantage of the system but, rather, they want their child (or grandchild) to be eligible to apply to various programs only available to those who receive governmental support. To guard against this issue and provide greater protection in general, children's trusts or grandchildren's trusts have grown in popularity.

As we delve into advanced planning tools, trusts are typically "irrevocable" to avoid issues of the assets being pulled back into the grantor's estate. Irrevocable trusts can be structured in a variety of ways for different beneficiaries — children, grandchildren, a spouse or a combination thereof. In addition, they are typically taxed in one of the following ways:

- **A grantor trust or an intentionally defective grantor trust.** All tax attributes flow back to the grantor which allows for the grantor to pay the income tax at the grantor's individual tax rate. When taxes are paid, they are not considered gifts making this another way to continue to move assets outside of the grantor's estate. Language can be added to the trust giving the trustee the ability to distribute funds to the grandparent (or parent) grantor to cover tax liabilities if there is an issue with paying taxes in any given year.

A grantor trust can also allow for greater flexibility in the future to swap assets. Imagine that Jack initially gifted shares of his business to a grantor trust and the business appreciated dramatically. From an estate tax planning perspective, this was wonderful because the business will pass estate tax free. However, because the business passes outside of Jack's taxable gross estate, his heirs do not get a step-up in basis and have to pay capital gains tax on the appreciation. If the trust was a grantor trust, when Jack exchanges the business assets for cash or another asset with a high tax basis prior to his death, there is no income tax triggered on the transfer. It is as if Jack sold the assets to himself. He could then die owning the business assets in his living trust which would get a step-up in basis — and the cash would pass estate tax free to his heirs.

- **A complex trust.** This type of trust is its own taxpayer and the income generated is taxed at the trust level; often at the highest rate. While this might appear undesirable at first blush, a complex trust provides flexibility to keep assets in trust for estate tax planning or asset protection purposes. If the trustee has the discretion to distribute income annually, the trustee can annually elect to distribute all of the income to the beneficiaries. Then the income taxes are paid at the individual beneficiary level instead of the trust level.

And while intentionally defective grantor trusts are often favored for their flexibility, there is a unique planning opportunity available with C-corp stock and complex trusts. As discussed further in Chapter 10, if the shareholder meets the necessary qualifications for a qualified small business stock capital gains exclusion, the shareholder may avoid capital gains on $10 million or more. If properly gifted to a complex trust for the benefit of a child, the same capital gains exclusion may be applicable when gifted to a complex trust which is a separate taxpayer. And if the shareholder has three children, capital gains exclusion is possible for the shareholder and each of the three separate trusts created for his children. Thus, leveraging estate planning and income tax planning can stack the capital gains exclusion for multiple individuals — saving the family millions of dollars in income taxes in addition to the estate tax saving benefits.

- **A simple trust.** Simple trusts require all income to be distributed annually. Income tax in connection with the trust activity is then picked up on the individual beneficiary's income tax return. This is typically how QTIP marital trusts are structured. In other instances, mandatory distributions of income can create challenges if a beneficiary is going through a contentious divorce or has creditors.

The tax treatment of the trust is a critical consideration and is identifying who the appropriate beneficiary or beneficiaries should be. Beneficiaries may include family members (spouse, children, grandchildren), friends or charitable organizations.

- **Children's gift trust / grandchildren's gift trust.** Once 529 planning has been maximized, if parents or grandparents wish to continue to provide for their loved ones, a gift trust is a wonderful tool. It provides a framework to protect the funds from potential creditors and in the instance of young adults — from themselves. No longer is there concern that a child will go to the bank at age 18 or 21 and withdraw a large amount of funds. The trust appoints a trustee to determine how and when distributions should be made to a beneficiary until the beneficiary reaches a particular age (often age 30 or 35). And the trust can be created for one beneficiary or multiple. A children's gift trust or a grandchildren's gift trust can be structured as an intentionally defective grantor trust, complex trust or simple trust. Most often, people are encouraged to use an intentionally defective grantor trust. But each trust is customized to meet the family's particular goals.

- **Spousal access trusts eliminate fear of financial setbacks.** Often, people are reluctant to make gifts because they fear a downturn in their financial fortunes. Even the wealthiest people may fear having to ask their children or grandchildren for money. But don't allow that to deter you from additional planning as other tools are available. In these situations, a spousal access trust is a wonderful planning tool. These are irrevocable trusts for the benefit of a spouse or a spouse in combination with descendants.

  Here's how it works: If Jack makes a gift to Diane, it becomes part of her taxable gross estate. However, if Jack makes the same gift to a spousal access trust for Diane's benefit, the transfer would use a portion of his lifetime gift exemption. The value of the gift, including appreciation, would be excluded from both of their estates. Read more about spousal access trusts and other advanced estate planning tools in Chapter 11.

- **Generation skipping trusts.** Grandchildren give you the ability to transfer wealth without creating an estate tax burden for your children. Generation skipping transfer (GST) trusts sometimes refer to passing assets to grandchildren so

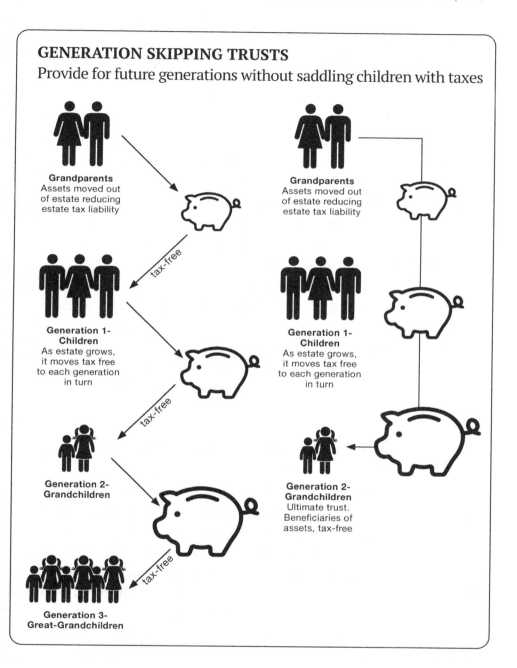

GENERATION SKIPPING TRUSTS
Provide for future generations without saddling children with taxes

Grandparents
Assets moved out
of estate reducing
estate tax liability

**Generation 1-
Children**
As estate grows,
it moves tax free
to each generation
in turn

**Generation 2-
Grandchildren**

**Generation 3-
Great-Grandchildren**

Grandparents
Assets moved out
of estate reducing
estate tax liability

**Generation 1-
Children**
As estate grows,
it moves tax free
to each generation
in turn

**Generation 2-
Grandchildren**
Ultimate trust.
Beneficiaries of
assets, tax-free

your children are not subject to estate taxes on the assets. You essentially "skip over" the child. In other planning scenarios, a GST trust merely refers to a trust that qualifies to pass estate tax free from generation to generation. The funds can be gifted to a trust for the benefit of children initially; structured in a way that allows funds to pass estate tax free from generation to generation.

This way the assets never become part of your children's estates and do not eat into their exemption or create unwanted estate tax liabilities. Trust language can also be written is such a way as to allow the beneficiary (a spouse or child) to have access to income generated by trust assets while still leaving those assets to pass estate tax free to the next generation (children or grandchildren).

The exemption level still applies to assets passed through GST trusts so it is important to remember that these levels fluctuate. In 2022, you could pass up to $12.06 million to your beneficiaries, including grandchildren, without paying estate taxes. However, in 2026, this level is currently scheduled to drop back to $5 million.

Grandchildren Are the Greatest Gift

As your family grows, each new generation is a new reason to update your estate plan to make sure your family has as much opportunity as possible to enjoy what previous generations have built. Laws governing the disposition of estates have long recognized the common urge to pass along the wealth you've managed to accumulate. For this reason, grandchildren present you and your estate planning attorney with a number of new tools to help you pass along as much of your estate as possible by minimizing taxes and sheltering your estate from time and money-consuming probate. The trust and gifting tools available to grandparents are both plentiful and powerful. Use them wisely.

Conversation Starters
Becoming Grandparents

Grandchildren come along at an intriguing time in most people's lives. Just when you are beginning to feel comfortable as empty-nesters, the nest welcomes new inhabitants. From an estate planning perspective, grandchildren bring new opportunities and new responsibilities for anyone who wants to extend the value of their hard-earned estate to a new generation. Here are some conversation starters that might prove valuable when beginning to think about how grandchildren change your estate planning needs.

1. **How helpful can we afford to be with the grandkids?**
   The key consideration is how much you can afford to give. This is where consultation with your financial planner or wealth advisor is critical to run an analysis of your needs. Grandchildren can get loans for college, if necessary — but loans for retirement are not available. Once you are certain there is more than enough to cover your lifestyle, you can look to give to children and grandchildren. Priorities are always important.

2. **How much do you think college will cost by the time our grandchildren are that age? Will they need help?**
   With education costs skyrocketing, your estate might best be spent planting an educational nest egg for your grandchildren. Having a conversation about educational expenses should lead to a discussion about how best to help your grandchildren with these anticipated expenses.

3. **Will our estate planning (as well as that of our**

children) benefit with some form of generation skipping trust?

Grandchildren give you another option when it comes to gifting assets. Helping another generation may improve your estate plan.

4. **How secure is our business? If there's a downturn, I really don't want to ask our grandchildren for money.**

   Family businesses present another group of concerns when it comes to adding grandchildren to your estate planning. Your attorney can advise you on how you can gift non-voting shares to ensure that you continue to maintain control.

5. **How comfortable are we leaving money to a minor grandchild? Are we sure they'll be ready to deal with it when they reach 18?**

   When structuring trusts to benefit grandchildren, it helps to think about protecting them from themselves. It would be a shame for them to lose their inheritance before they are old enough to appreciate what you've left them.

6. **Where did the time go?**

   You may never have thought of yourself as grandparents, but time flies by. Your children begin to have children of their own and priorities shift. Keep your estate plan up to date so future generations can benefit.

Chapter 10
Diane Starts a Business

Big changes were in the air at Jack and Diane's Fox Valley home. With the children all gone, grandchildren growing more independent by the day, and Jack still running a successful business empire, Diane felt a bit stuck. It seemed she had spent her lifetime building things for other people. She'd made a fine home for Jack and the kids. She had turned herself into the perfect business wife, always ready to host 18 unexpected business guests at a moment's notice. She wasn't complaining. It had been a good life. But, the embers of ambition that had burned bright when she first met Jack, still smoldered. Diane wanted to build something she could call her own.

One afternoon when the house was quiet, Diane started to write down some business ideas. On one side of the sheet of paper she wrote all the talents she'd developed. On the other side she wrote down the things she'd likely have to give up in order to start a new business. Near the bottom of that list was "time with Jack."

As the hours ticked by, a vision began to take shape. She remembered all the business parties she had pulled together for Jack's business and realized how much she'd learned about staging a successful event. She knew the right chefs to use, how to get people there and how to make an evening "magical" and "memorable." Why couldn't she start an event planning company? Although she'd worked with good event planners who knew how to stage grand charity balls, she never had found one that knew how to stage intimate business events.

She called her best friend, Sherry, to see if she would have any interest in partnering in such an endeavor. Of course Sherry was in. Just like Diane, she had a lot of experience staging business events for her successful husband. Years later, both women looked back on that phone call as one of the most fateful of their lives.

Deciding How to Structure a New Business

A new business is an asset that becomes part of a person's estate. As it grows and increases in value, it adds significant estate tax implications. In addition to considering the tax liabilities of the business, there are potentially significant liability concerns that could expose other estate assets to forfeiture if the business is not properly structured from the beginning. Too often a person jumps into a new business venture with eyes closed to everything except what they believe they have to do to build a successful business. Diane and Sherry were in a slightly different position than most entrepreneurs in the early stages of building a business. They already had significant assets to protect and had estates with significant estate tax concerns.

Everyone who starts a business dreams of success, but with success comes decisions that people like Diane and Sherry have to face from the very beginning. Chief among these decisions is how to structure the business for both legal and tax purposes. There are different business entities that all entrepreneurs need to consider to ensure the entity best meets their individual situations. Diane also needs to consider her family's success and other assets when making this decision.

— *Sole proprietorships*

This is overwhelmingly the way most businesses start because it is the simplest and easiest way to organize a business. A sole proprietorship is one person doing business under a fictitious or assumed name. It could be Diane Lane doing business as Fox River Events. Fox River Events is the name of a business that is really a person, Diane Lane.

As a sole proprietor:

- Diane does not have to file any paperwork with the state, since sole proprietorships are not subject to state laws regarding their organization or operation. However, it's a good idea to file a DBA (doing business as) with the county in which the business is located to protect your company name and identity.

- There is no need for a separate Federal Employer Identification Number (FEIN) and no annual maintenance payments to the state to maintain an organizational status. Indeed, Fox River Events never even has to file separate tax forms.

- All profits and losses are reported on the owner's individual tax return.

The attraction of sole proprietorships is simplicity. However, in situations such as Diane's, there are serious drawbacks, especially when it comes to asset protection. If her business is sued, she is the liable party, putting all other assets she owns or co-owns at risk of an adverse judgement.

— *General partnership*

Imagine Diane and Sherry put together a simple agreement

stating that they plan to embark on this business together. A general partnership is a business arrangement where two or more individuals (or businesses) agree to share in all assets, profits and liabilities of a jointly owned business venture. It is simple in design and does not require any formal filings with a secretary of state either at formation or on an annual basis. The general partnership will need to obtain a business tax identification number (FEIN) and file an annual informational return with the IRS. The profits and losses of the general partnership will "flow through" to its partners proportionate to their ownership. However, a major drawback of a general partnership is that the partners agree they will be liable for the business. In other words, liabilities of the business can extend to their individual assets. For this reason, educated business partners will look to a different type of business structure to formalize their partnership in a way that would provide greater asset protection for their personal assets.

— *Limited partnership*

A limited partnership has two types of partners — (1) one or more general partners who manage the partnership and are potentially exposed to some level of liability; and (2) one or more limited partners who own equity in the business, do not have a management function and are insulated from liability.

When partners own a business together, a limited partnership agreement limits the liability of the non-managing partners who serve as the "silent" limited investors. However, the general partner has unlimited liability for risks and losses of the partnership. In other words, with management rights come potential liability. Generally, this business structure is used by real estate developers, doctors, lawyers, architects, veterinarians, accountants and other professional partnerships.

— *Family limited partnership*

Because limited partnerships provide such outstanding structures for estate planning, they have given rise to an additional category of family limited partnerships (FLP), which maximize wealth transfer and protect personal assets.

Basically, an FLP is a business entity where family members invest in a business opportunity and own shares in relationship to the amount individual members invest.

If Jack's family decides to purchase a $1 million apartment building, five family members could agree to invest $100,000 each making each one a 20% limited partner. The remaining $500,000 could then be financed through a mortgage loan taken out in the name of the Smith Family Limited Partnership.

However, this form of partnership can also be used as a valuable estate planning tool allowing parents to begin transferring assets to their heirs, over time, in the form of limited partnership interests.

Jack could start Jack's Family Limited Partnership funded with $4 million worth of his assets. In an effort to provide some level of asset protection for the general partners, often a Limited Liability Company (LLC) or S Corporation is created to act as the general partner. The LLC may be initially owned and controlled by Jack's living trust and Diane's living trust. The LLC acting as the general partner owns 1% of the FLP and retains 1% of the assets, or $40,000. Initially, their separate living trusts own the 99% limited partnership interest of the FLP. However, over time, Jack and Diane can begin "gifting" their ownership interest in the FLP at a discount, thereby reducing the size of their taxable gross estate.

Discounted shares mean more value from every gift. Limited partners who have no management rights are deemed of less value than partners who can actually manage the assets. The same is true for limited partners who own only a minority interest in the business (49% or less) and privately held businesses where there is no secondary market or limited sale opportunity for the ownership interests. When valuing a limited partnership interest, you can take discounts to account for what the IRS characterizes as a "lack of marketability" or "lack of control." Discounts can vary dramatically, depending on the structure of the partnership and the mix of assets but can range from 15% to 40%.

Conservatively, a 25% discount means every limited partnership interest that has an initial fair market value of $1,000 would have a value of $750 when you take discounts for lack of marketability and lack of control. The discount allows Jack to transfer interests worth 25% more than their fair market valuation. In a given year, Jack and Diane can gift the annual exclusion amount of $16,000 each or $32,000 as a married couple. Rather than giving each child 32 limited partnership interests a year (valued at $32,000), they can gift 42 limited partnership interests to each child without exceeding the annual gifting limit. Suddenly, $42,000 of Jack and Diane's wealth is transferred each year to every child, tax free. Best of all, the assets remain in the Jack's Family Limited Partnership under Jack and Diane's indirect control, while transferring wealth to their children.

Limited Partnerships at a glance:

- **Formation**: A "Certificate of Formation" is filed with the Secretary of State.

- **Organization:** A partnership agreement should be created and agreed to by all partners.
- **Management:** A general partner is selected by the partners and is responsible for the operation of the partnership.
- **Employer identification:** A Federal Employer Identification Number (FEIN) is required.
- **Annual fees:** Annual maintenance fees and annual meeting minutes are required.
- **Taxation:** All taxable profits flow through to the individual partners according to the partnership agreement.
- **Asset protection:** Liability is limited for the limited partners (often 99% ownership interest), but not for the general partner (often 1% ownership interest).

— *Using corporate structures to protect assets* —

The key to asset protection, as it is for estate tax minimization, is to put the asset, in this case your new business, into a separate entity. New entrepreneurs are often surprised at the number of structural options available to them.

When properly maintained, business entities are separate and distinct legal entities. They are owned by shareholders, so if the entity goes bankrupt or loses a lawsuit, only the business assets are at risk. But, unless a business owner has personally guaranteed corporate debt, the business owner's individual assets, outside of the business, remain safe.

— *C Corporations* —

C-corps are relatively easy to set up and are the most different from a sole proprietor. As is true with other forms of incorporation, a C-corp is owned by shareholders. The dual taxation of C-corps often made them unattractive business structures. However, the Small Business Stock Capital Gains Exclusion makes C-corp an attractive structure for the right type of business. Specifically, if the C-corp and shareholder meet the necessary qualifications, the shareholder can exclude the greater of (1) 10 times the shareholder's tax basis in the stock; or (2) $10 million of capital gain. Eligible C-corps are often start-ups, and when estate planning is properly incorporated with the use of complex trusts, the small business stock capital gains exclusion can apply to trusts created for the benefit of various family members.

C Corporations at a glance:

- **Filings with state:** Articles of Incorporation must be filed with the state. At a certain point, a C-corp may have to register with the SEC.
- **Formal structure:** Bylaws should be developed outlining the corporate structure and how the enterprise is to be managed. A board of directors should be formed.
- **Stock:** Stock certificates should be issued.
- **Employer identification:** Obtain a separate Federal Employers Identification Number (FEIN).
- **Taxation:** The corporation must file its own tax return separate from the founders and shareholders. The corporation will be taxed at an entity level and individual shareholders will also be taxed on their earnings from stock appreciation.
- **Yearly board meetings:** In most states, yearly meetings and minutes of those meetings are required to maintain C-corp status.
- **Fees:** Annual maintenance fees must be paid to the state and annual reports must be filed.

- **Sustainability:** If one shareholder dies or declares bankruptcy, the shareholder agreement could provide guidance on what the remaining shareholders may do — or might be required to do.
- **Asset protection:** Any corporation provides asset protection since it is a separate entity from the shareholders. However, if you do not adhere to the rules of a corporation — perhaps by mixing corporate assets with personal assets or not holding yearly board meetings — creditors could possibly pierce the corporation's "veil" and reach the underlying stock. If a creditor ever reaches the underlying stock in the corporation, the creditor can potentially take control over the entity and force distributions to be made to that creditor in payment of debt.

— S Corporations

People often look at S-corps as a "quick fix" to form a new entity. Filing fees are often lower than those for a C-corp, and there are significant tax advantages. This type of corporation eliminates the possibility of double-taxation of corporate profits while offering shareholders the benefits of taxation as a partnership.

All taxable profits, or losses, flow through to the shareholders and are reported on the shareholders tax returns. This minimizes taxes since a substantial amount of shareholder income is distributed as dividends without withholding or self-employment taxes. If the shareholder is also drawing a salary from the S-corp, withholding taxes are paid on that portion of their income.

S-corps are limited to 100 or fewer shareholders and offer

minimum asset protection. Additionally, if an LLC files the appropriate paperwork with the IRS, it can elect to be taxed as an S-corp. This is often an attractive option for service businesses, allowing the minimization of taxes while enjoying some asset protection.

S Corporations at a glance:

- **Filings with state:** Articles of Incorporation must be filed with the state.
- **Formal structure:** Bylaws should be developed outlining the corporate structure and how the enterprise is to be managed.
- **Stock:** Stock certificates should be issued.
- **Employer identification:** Obtain a separate Federal Employers Identification Number (FEIN) and an S-corp election must be filed with the IRS.
- **Taxation:** Taxable profits flow through to the stockholders in the form of dividends so there is no withholding or self-employment taxes.
- **Fees:** Annual maintenance fees must be paid to the state and annual reports filed.
- **Sustainability:** If one shareholder dies or declares bankruptcy, the shareholder agreement could provide guidance on what the remaining shareholders may do — or might be required to do.
- **Asset protection:** Any corporation provides asset protection since it is a separate entity from the shareholders. However, if a creditor ever reaches the underlying stock in the corporation, the creditor can potentially take control over the entity and force distributions to be made.

— *Limited Liability Company (LLC)* —

An LLC combines the personal liability protection of a corporation and the tax benefits and simplicity of a partnership. Owners, referred to as "members," are not personally liable for a company's debts or liabilities unless they personally guarantee a debt. This means LLCs offer the following advantages:

- No corporate level taxation since all taxes flow through to the individual members
- No personal liability
- Flexibility in management and allocation of profits and losses.

From a management perspective, LLCs can be either manager-managed or member-managed. People often follow the manager-managed model in order to gain additional asset protection because it offers further separation of members from the business entity. However, whether manager or member, most states do not extend limited liability protection to carry out an LLC's fraudulent acts.

In many states, LLCs offer enhanced asset protection over corporations because they offer a "charging order protection." A creditor of a corporation may be able to reach the underlying stock in the business and gain control over the entity. In contrast, in many states, like Delaware, a charging order is the exclusive remedy for a debtor of an LLC. In this way, a creditor could only receive a charging order which would provide that if a distribution is made to a member, the creditor can reach it. However, the creditor cannot force distributions to be made.

Typically, an LLC is taxed as a partnership whereby all income would flow through to the members' personal returns through K-1s, the form provided to shareholders to include with their personal tax returns. However, as previously noted, an LLC may also file an election to be taxed as an S-corp. If the entity was a service business and wanted to avoid the additional withholding, an S-corp election may be a wonderful fit.

Limited Liability Company at a glance:

- **Filings with state:** Certificate of Formation must be filed with the state.
- **Formal structure:** There should be a formal operating agreement among the members.
- **Employer identification:** Obtain a separate Federal Employers Identification Number (FEIN) unless the entity is 100% owned by a single member and is considered a disregarded entity.
- **Taxation:** As a partnership, all taxable income and losses flow through to the members as dividends. The appropriate taxes are paid on the member level. As noted above, an LLC may also file an S-election to be taxed as an S-corp.
- **Fees:** Annual maintenance fees must be paid to the state and annual reports must be filed.
- **Sustainability:** If one member dies or declares bankruptcy, the operating agreement would provide guidance on what the remaining members may do — or might be required to do.
- **Asset protection:** An LLC provides substantial asset protection since it is a separate entity from the shareholders and the charging order protection can further increase the asset protection.

— *Series LLC*

When LLCs were first introduced, many people and practitioners looked to put everything into the LLC. However, this quickly led to an "overstuffed entity" problem. The LLC would protect the individual from the outside world but would subject, or open, all assets in the LLC to a potential claim.

Imagine having one LLC with three different real estate properties. The LLC protects those properties from creditors going after assets not in the LLC, but if a liability arose with one property in the LLC, the liability has a domino effect and can take down the other assets even though they are protected in the LLC.

In 1996, Delaware was the first state to adopt and recognize LLCs. Since then, several states have followed suit. To maximize asset protection, some businesses form Series LLCs to distribute risk among different entities linked together in the same way a large corporation can have subsidiaries. These Series LLCs are not allowed in every state.

The concept of a Series LLC is to segregate risk within separate entities without the cost of setting up multiple legal entities.

In states allowing Series LLCs, the articles of formation specifically allow for unlimited segregation of membership interests, assets and operations into independent series. Each of these series operate independently with separate banking, management, books and records. Each may also have different members and managers. The key is that liabilities are contained within each individual series. Other series in the chain are protected against risks borne by other series.

The Series LLC concept is especially attractive to real estate investors who place ownership of individual buildings into different series. In this manner, though all the buildings are held within the same corporate structure, the owners of each building are protected from liabilities incurred by other buildings.

Series LLCs at a glance:

- **Filings with state:** Formed the same way as a traditional LLC. In states where this structure is allowed, the articles of formation state that series LLCs are permitted.
- **Formal structure:** Often there is a master LLC with its own operating agreement. Each series operates independently of the others.
- **Employer identification:** Obtain a Federal Employers Identification Number (FEIN) for the master LLC, and often for each additional series.
- **Taxation:** As a partnership, all taxable income and losses from each series flow through to the members as dividends. The appropriate taxes are paid on the member level.
- **Fees:** Annual maintenance fees must be paid to the state and annual reports must be filed for the master LLC and each series.
- **Sustainability:** If one member dies or declares bankruptcy, the operating agreement would provide guidance on what the remaining members may do, or might be required to do.
- **Asset protection:** Each individual entity in the series has its own risks that are segregated from other entities in the series. If one series suffers a loss or adverse legal judgement, the liability is limited to that particular series.

How Business Structure Affects Estate Planning

Since tax minimization and asset protection is at the heart of most estate planning, family limited partnerships can be extremely useful, making it easier to pass more money to heirs without paying gift taxes or surrendering management of the assets. However, the fact of the matter is that any business entity that puts your new business into an entity separate from your estate will be helpful in minimizing estate taxes when the time comes.

The most important consideration is your personal estate planning objectives. If asset protection is most important, a limited partnership or LLC might prove a good fit. If tax minimization is your primary concern, an S-corp (or LLC taxed as an S-corp) might prove more valuable. A good estate planner can help guide you in these important decisions.

Similar to discounts afforded for limited partnership interests, a corporation or LLC can also provide a mechanism for wealth transfer. Specifically, a corporation (or S-corp) or LLC could have two classes of owners — voting and nonvoting interests. When properly designed, discounts can be taken on nonvoting interests for lack of marketability and lack of control. In this way, with knowledge and creativity, almost any business structure can lend itself to estate planning and wealth transfer.

— *Diane's choice*

Diane and Sherry spent a lot of time considering all their options because both had considerable family assets to protect. Their most important secondary concern was building a business that they could easily step away from at some future point. They both wanted to build a sustainable business that helped them minimize taxes while protecting their family assets.

Eventually, they decided an LLC was the way to go. It was fairly easy to set up, provided a separate business entity that would not entangle their family assets, and its corporate structure allowed them to agree on how the business would be operated and develop a sustainable organization that could outlive them both.

4. **How much risk can you tolerate?**

   Every business requires investments in time and money. How much are you willing to risk in both? Understanding your risk tolerance will go a long way toward determining the kind of business you build.

5. **Should you involve other family members in this new business?**

   If a family partnership appeals to you, it may impact estate planning conversations and how you choose to transfer assets during your lifetime and at death.

6. **How big could this thing grow?**

   Are you dreaming big? You may well be starting a business that could have a number of spin-offs in the future. Make sure your selected business structure can easily accommodate dynamic growth.

7. **What will this business do to your current estate plan? Is your business interest held through a revocable living trust?**

   Perhaps it's time to call your estate planning attorney before finalizing your business plans. And, at the very least, make certain your business interests are titled in the name of your revocable living trust to help avoid probate.

Chapter 11
Jack and Diane's Estate Grows

Diane and Sherry worked hard. Jack and his partners worked hard. Both their businesses were resounding successes. Money was rolling in, although they had paid a heavy price in lost time together.

Time passed in the blink of an eye. The kids were doing well. Katie joined Jack in his business and had proven to be an astute investor. Ethan was determined to save the world and seemed to spend every waking hour on an airplane visiting local governments to advise them on effective climate change regulations. Whitney was moving up the ranks at a high-profile magazine and raising amazing kids herself. Life was pretty good, and their estate was growing faster and larger than they had ever anticipated. It was time to sit down again with their estate planning attorney.

By now, estate taxes were a very real concern. Jack and Diane's estate had grown large enough to ensure a healthy inheritance for their children. Until now they were primarily concerned with making sure their family would be able to survive comfortably if one or both of them died. Now they had true wealth and were concerned with passing on the assets they had accumulated during a lifetime of hard work, smart investments and good choices.

As they sat in their attorney's office, they both seemed lost in thought. Jack was wondering what would happen to everything he had earned along the way. Diane was thinking back to the first time they had visited this office. At that time they carried no documents or briefcases. There were no statements of investment accounts or large properties to consider. They weren't concerned with the succession planning of their businesses or particularly worried about federal estate taxes. They were just two young adults ready to start a life together and determined to do the right things when it came to their finances. So many years ago, life was simple. Now things were different.

How Viewpoints Change

Most people, early on in life, focus on building a solid foundation for future growth and ensuring their kids' futures are protected in case of an unexpected tragedy. Later in life, people focus their efforts on minimizing estate taxes and passing on assets without jeopardizing their own future comfort. This is exactly where Jack and Diane have found themselves.

At this point, all of their assets were in revocable trusts. They could certainly gift considerable assets to their children and set up a series of irrevocable trusts to move assets out of their control. However, both Jack and Diane had become accustomed to a certain lifestyle and wanted to make sure they could continue living this way as the future unfolded. If they moved too much of their wealth to the control of others, they ran the risk of having to ask their children for help in the future, a situation neither wanted to face.

The solution began with a meeting with their team of advisors before undertaking any big picture moves. The team ran in-depth financial projections to help them understand what it would take to continue living the lifestyle they had earned. Like flight attendants say on airplanes, "Make sure your mask is secure before helping anyone else." The goal is to make certain that Jack and Diane's needs are appropriately met, focusing on their goals before developing changes to their existing estate plan.

Both Jack and Diane wanted to care for their grandchildren's education. Diane was especially concerned with maintaining their Fox River Valley home and the winter home they'd built in Palm Springs. Jack was more concerned with maintaining control of his business until daughter Katie was ready to take over. He also wanted to ensure his control of the many commercial real estate assets he'd accumulated over the years.

As they were about to learn, Jack and Diane had been building an estate plan that mirrored the plans for a solid house. The foundation was the pour over wills, revocable living trusts, powers of attorney for healthcare, and powers of attorney for property. Jack and Diane built this foundation to leverage tax planning, avoid the courts and provide asset protection for beneficiaries. The plan was designed to protect themselves and their children in case one of them died prematurely.

The first floor of the plan included an irrevocable life insurance trust (ILIT). These trusts were designed to pay the beneficiaries enough to continue their lifestyle at the time and take care of anticipated estate taxes with tax free dollars. Jack remembered his bygone fears that Ethan could possibly fall into a life of drugs and excess, so he designated a business partner as the trustee of his ILIT with detailed instructions concerning Ethan's ability to access available assets. ILIT's are discussed in more detail in Chapter 6.

As Jack's business prospered and they accumulated enough assets to ensure their children's well-being in the event of their early death, Jack and Diane built the second story of their estate planning house using gift trusts for both children. These were also irrevocable gifts based on yearly and lifetime gifting limits.

By this point in their estate planning process, Jack and Diane had done quite a bit to ensure their children were well cared for in the event of their premature death or disability. However, now their children were successful in their own right and really didn't need their parent's further help. The focus of Jack and Diane's estate planning had shifted to tax minimization on a large and rapidly growing estate.

As they'd seen throughout their lives, the key to tax minimization was to get as many assets out of their control as possible, primarily using trusts. Now they needed to make sure each had enough to continue living their life in the manner they desired. To build the third story of their estate planning house they needed to turn to a group of versatile trusts as protectors of their interests in life as they are after death.

Trusts to Protect Interests

As we have discussed, trusts are fundamental to every estate plan. They become more important to people who have generated significant wealth in their lives as a way to protect interests today and ensure wishes are carried out after death. Let's explore common trusts used to accomplish this.

— *Spousal access trusts*

A spousal access trust is an irrevocable gift trust created for the benefit of a spouse or a spouse and children. When people look at making larger gifts, they have concerns about their future

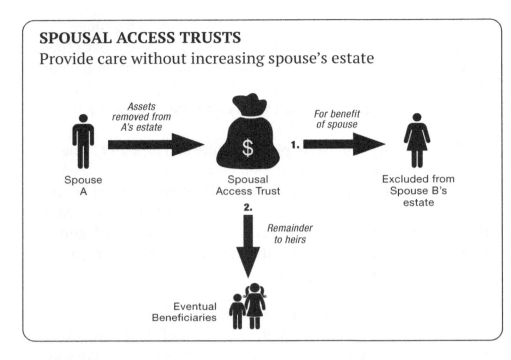

SPOUSAL ACCESS TRUSTS
Provide care without increasing spouse's estate

Assets removed from A's estate

Spouse A

Spousal Access Trust

For benefit of spouse

1.

Excluded from Spouse B's estate

2.

Remainder to heirs

Eventual Beneficiaries

needs. Reluctance remains even when a wealth advisor provides forecast modeling to assure a couple there is more than enough to provide for their future needs. No one wants to be in a position where they need to ask a child for financial help.

Even couples who have made some gifts to their children and still want to do more estate tax planning are not comfortable with the idea of transferring so much wealth into a trust for their kids too soon. This is when they consider a spousal access trust. This type of trust allows them to move assets outside of their taxable gross estate while still allowing for the funds to be available for a significant other should circumstances or needs change.

If Jack were to transfer assets to Diane or to her living trust, he's simply moving assets from his taxable gross estate to Diane's taxable gross estate. However, if Jack gifted outside of their taxable gross estate, he could move those assets outside of their taxable gross estate while still providing flexibility for Diane to access the funds if she were to need them. In an ideal world, the spouse would not need to use the funds and the assets would grow inside of the trust and eventually pass estate tax free to the children. But just in case, this type of trust allows a spouse accessibility to the money during their lifetime. Whatever is left over passes estate tax free to the children or grandchildren when the beneficiary spouse dies.

When a spouse is a beneficiary of a trust, IRS regulations provide that such trust is automatically an intentionally defective grantor trust. In this way, additional wealth transfer benefits are already built into the planning whereby the grantor pays the income tax liabilities in connection with assets in the trust. By doing so, if a tax liability arises for assets in a trust Jack created for Diane's benefit, additional funds are moved out of Jack's taxable gross estate and the assets, which will pass estate tax free inside of the trust, continue to grow. As previously discussed, the trust may also include a provision which would allow the trustee the discretion to distribute assets from the trust to the grantor to help cover the tax liabilities. Ideally, Jack would have sufficient cash flow to cover the income taxes. Should that change, the trust can distribute funds to Jack to cover income taxes in connection with the trust liabilities.

Spousal access trusts grow in popularity when estate tax limits are in danger of dropping as they are currently scheduled to do in 2026 (or possibly sooner if the current estate and gift tax exemptions change). Both in 2012 when the exemption faced threat of changing and in today's current uncertain estate tax climate, spousal access trusts are one of the most popular planning tools for couples to implement. In addition, when clients are contemplating significantly larger lifetime gifts of $24.12 million ($12.06 million by each spouse), they feel a greater level of comfort moving forward with wealth transfer planning if they know there is a back-up plan which would allow a spouse to access the funds.

Spousal access trusts grow in popularity when estate tax limits are in danger of dropping

Theoretically, Jack could create a trust for Diane's benefit and Diane could create one for the benefit of Jack and the children. One trust is for the benefit of a spouse and the other is for the benefit of the spouse and children at the same time. The beneficiaries are slightly modified to avoid the IRS's "reciprocal trust doctrine." In addition, other material terms of the trust should be modified including:

- Beneficiaries
- Trustees
- Distribution standards for income and principal
- Power of appointment
- Ultimate beneficiaries
- Date trust is created
- Type or amount of asset gifted to trust

Unfortunately, if the trusts are considered reciprocal in nature, the IRS can unwind the gifting and pull the gifted assets back into their taxable gross estates. Thus, when engaging in planning that is similar in any fashion between parties, the trusts can be similar in nature but must have material different provisions so that they are not deemed to be reciprocal by the IRS.

For many people, even those with an uber high net worth, the idea of suddenly making a large irrevocable gift to a trust (even for the benefit of a spouse) requires some time to process. To help them feel more comfortable, people are encouraged to consider the implications of planning and walk through various scenarios with their advisory team. In addition, people often appreciate the two-step approach. Imagine Jack and Diane begin the process with Jack creating a trust for the benefit of Diane and gifting some level of assets to it. Once they have time to see how the process works, witness appreciation of the assets outside of their estate and understand the implications, they are more inclined to doing more similar planning on a larger scale. Perhaps Diane later creates a trust for the benefit of Jack and the kids utilizing their remaining lifetime exemption of $24.12 million.

— *Qualified personal residence trusts (QPRT)* —

Many people are concerned about staying in their own homes even when those homes have been gifted to the children as part of their advanced estate planning. Qualified personal residence trusts (QPRT) establish a tax-minimization protocol for gifting houses while ensuring the right to continue living in them.

You can place up to two residences in a properly structured QPRT. These trusts can be funded with a primary residence, a vacation or secondary residence or a fractional interest in either. A QPRT funded with both the Fox River Valley primary residence and their Palm Springs winter home would give Diane the domicile security she wants and significant tax advantages.

In terms of Diane's peace of mind, the QPRT would give her the right to live rent-free for a specified term (perhaps 10 years) in a primary or secondary home she gifted to her children. She maintains a "retained interest." Upon the expiration of the term, ownership of the home transfers to the beneficiaries as "remainder beneficiaries." Because Diane retains an interest, the value of the gift is reduced. Imagine that Diane transfers a $1 million property to a QPRT and retains the ability to live there rent free for 10 years. The $1 million gift is discounted to take into consideration her retained interest / ability to live in the property.

Upon the term expiration, Diane can continue to live in the home paying rent as if it were an arms-length transaction. In other words, her rent payment would be in line with market rates. The rent would be paid to the trust that owns the homes, and whose beneficiaries are Jack and Diane's children. Since rent paid to the trust is an arm's length transaction, it is not considered a gift and can provide another way to continue to transfer wealth. And, if the QPRT (or sub-trust which holds title to the property) is structured as an intentionally defective grantor trust where all income tax liabilities flow back to the grantor, it is as if Diane is paying rent to herself and the rental payments are income tax free. Read more about intentionally defective grantor trusts on Chapter 9.

If Diane dies prior to the specified term of the QPRT, the property is pulled back into her estate. QPRTs are generally attractive in high interest rate environments. However, even when interest rates are low, clients may look to QPRTs as an efficient way to transfer assets without disrupting one's lifestyle. In other words, Diane's lifestyle and cash flow are not affected by gifting the home. And the trust has appropriate protections in place requiring that she be able to stay in the property for as long as she (or Jack) wishes — provided they pay the appropriate "rent."

The QPRT can also offer other significant tax minimization advantages to Jack and Diane. By gifting fractional interests, you are often able to get discounts for valuation purposes. Again, owning fractional interest does not give you the right to sell a property, so is not worth as much as a full ownership stake. A fractional interest in property worth $1 million dollars may only be valued at $750,000 – and with a QPRT, the value of that gift is further decreased by retained interest / ability to live in the property rent-free for a specific period. Further, appreciation in the value of the home will not be in a decedent's estate, lowering the value of their estate and the corresponding estate tax bill.

The only down side to a QPRT relates to the risk that the Grantor may die during the trust term (the transaction is then unwound) – and that it is difficult to effectively allocate generation skipping transfer tax exemption. In this way, it remains an effective vehicle to transfer wealth to the next generation but the value of the gift is often included in the beneficiary's taxable gross estate.

— *Grantor retained annuity trust* —

Grantor retained annuity trusts (GRATs) work in a similar way as QPRTs, allowing a grantor to move assets into a trust, removing them from their estate while still receiving income in the form of an annuity from the assets.

Under a GRAT, assets are contributed to a trust, and for a specified term the grantor receives an annuity. At the expiration of the specified term, the balance is held for the benefit of the trust beneficiaries. If the grantor dies before the trust term expires, the remaining assets become part of their taxable estate and do not transfer to the beneficiaries.

Imagine that Jack has a commercial real estate property worth $2.4 million. The property is held through an LLC, and when discounts for lack of marketability and lack of control are implemented, the discounted value is $2 million. The property in question generates $200,000 in cash flow annually. If Jack transfers the property to a GRAT and retains the right to receive the cash flow for 10 years ($200,000 x 10), the value of the gift is reduced by the amount he receives as an annuity. Suddenly the value of the gift is $0. This is known as a "zeroed-out" GRAT, whereby the amount contributed to the trust is equal to the present value of the future annuity payments to Jack.

GRATs are often most attractive in low interest rate environments, but can work favorably in any environment for the right property and the right person.

GRATs are often most attractive in low interest rate environments

It is easy to see how a GRAT could be very attractive to wealthy individuals who own commercial real estate or other assets generating income and expected to appreciate. By placing these assets in a GRAT, the value of the asset is frozen for estate planning purposes and the grantor is still able to enjoy the fruits of the investment for a specified term while moving the asset outside of their estate.

Similar to a QPRT, often the only down side to a GRAT relates to the risk of a grantor dying during the trust term (the transaction is then unwound). It is also difficult to allocate a generation skipping transfer tax exemption. In this way, it remains an effective vehicle to transfer wealth to the next generation. However, because it is difficult to allocate GST, the value of the gift is often included in the beneficiary's taxable gross estate.

— *Freeze technique*

From time to time, instead of gifting an asset, people want to "freeze" the value of the asset. A freeze technique allows the current value to remain in your estate while moving all future appreciation outside of your taxable gross estate.

Imagine Diane believes her party planning business is going to appreciate dramatically. If the current value of Diane's portion of the business is $1 million, she could "sell" the business to an intentionally defective grantor trust in exchange for a promissory note. The trust would now hold title to the ownership interest in the business and Diane's estate would have the promissory note. The promissory note can provide for interest-only payments with the entire principal due at the end of a specified term in the form of a balloon payment. When Diane sells the note to the intentionally defective grantor trust, it is as if she is selling it to herself so there are no income tax implications in connection with the sale (or interest payments made on the note). The transaction freezes the business interest at the current value of $1 million.

Treasury regulations suggest that the trust must be seeded with at least 10% of the asset value. That can be done in the form of a "gift" or, perhaps, the trust has other assets that can constitute the "seed."

Jack and Diane had reached a fortunate stage of their lives when their estates were growing by leaps and bounds. With proper estate planning, they were able to use their hard-earned money to make sure their children would be cared for if something happened to them. Then they were able to solidify their growing estate without taxes taking too large a bite or allowing assets to be threatened by future creditors.

At this stage of the estate planning process, the most important conversations relate to how much money either spouse needs to live on versus how many assets need to be moved out of their estate for tax minimization purposes. Strong consideration should also be given to the nature of the assets you've accumulated, especially how likely they are to appreciate. These types of conversations will help guide tax minimization and asset transfer efforts.

1. **I know you never want to ask the kids for financial support. So let's consider how much money you need to maintain your lifestyle?**
   This is a conversation concerning both of you since no one knows which spouse will survive the other.

2. **Is it important that you have access to your real estate properties?**
   Most people want to maintain control of their primary or secondary residence. However, you can gift the property but still retain the ability to live there or elect to sell the current property to buy a new home. And gifting real property (instead of cash) does not have an impact on your cash flow or accessibility to financial resources.

3. **Some of the things we own are likely to be worth a lot more very soon. If our assets appreciate as expected, how does that affect our potential estate tax liabilities?**
   By moving assets likely to increase in value, you move not only the current value but also all future appreciation outside

of your estate. You can freeze asset values while passing the appreciation of the assets to the next generation.

4. **Could the children take care of themselves if we were no longer around?**
   Certainly, you'll want your children taken care of, but the saying, "save yourself first" also applies. Make sure your estate plan doesn't put you in the position of asking your children for support just because you had an overly aggressive tax minimization plan.

5. **Is our estate plan sufficient to handle our new financial circumstances?**
   As your life changes so should your estate plan. When your assets grow, make sure your estate plan keeps pace.

6. **How much control of my business do I want to maintain?**
   Always a dicey subject but one you'll need to confront as you plan to pass assets on to the next generation. Unfortunately, many effective estate planning techniques require that you part with control in some fashion. And there is no need to do everything at once — consider making small modifications to ownership over time to make certain you are comfortable.

Chapter 12
Jack and Diane Have Charitable Interests

As Diane's business continued to flourish, she found herself in a position unique to successful entrepreneurs. With a management team in place, she now had time to pursue her charitable interests. Diane had grown fond of the Chicago Art Institute. She spent a rare off-day there and marveled at the world-class art collection and the way she learned something new every time she went there. She especially enjoyed the weekly ARTe stories she received as part of her membership and silently vowed to help make these stories available to future generations of Chicagoans. Diane was also a big supporter of the Crohn's and Colitis Foundation since her son, Ethan, was diagnosed with Crohn's Disease when he was in college. Ethan had managed the disease surprisingly well, but Diane hoped a cure could soon be found.

Jack had been so focused on building his business that he hadn't had the time to be involved with outside activities, but when one of his top managers had lost a young son to pediatric cancer, he became involved with Advocate Children's Hospital.

Jack and Diane had both worked hard their whole lives to build successful businesses. Their children were settled in their own families and were financially secure, especially in light of the gifts they had already received from Jack and Diane. However, there was still a lot of money left in their estate, much of it potentially liable to future estate taxes.

Jack and Diane decided to leave a lasting philanthropic legacy — some non-profits were about to get substantial gifts.

The Two Sides of Giving

Countless people find charitable giving an incredibly satisfying tool in their estate planning efforts. For this reason, there is a distinction between "qualitative" and "quantitative" giving. Qualitative giving involves providing support because it makes you feel good to support non-profits close to your heart. Quantitative giving entails making gifts and bequests to minimize estate and income taxes.

The fact that people make charitable gifts for different reasons shouldn't obscure the value of charity in a good estate plan. Whether given to satisfy your heart or your tax minimization plans — or both — charitable giving can be invaluable if done in the right way.

When it comes to quantitative giving, it is especially important to be strategic. The manner in which you leave your gifts or bequests will go a long way to leveraging the amount of the gifts you can make. You should meet with your estate planning professional before making one or more charitable organizations a part of your estate planning. Both your ability to give and the tax planning benefits you receive depend on the way you make your gifts, and you'll want to maximize both the size of your gifts and the tax minimization benefits.

Is It Better to Give during Your Lifetime or after Death?

People often ponder whether it is better to make lifetime transfers or make bequests after death. It's actually lifetime transfers that give you both qualitative and quantitative benefits:

- *From a qualitative viewpoint,* you get to see the benefits of your giving. There are few things in life more heartwarming than seeing your hard-earned money make a difference in other people's lives and the community at large.

- *From a quantitative viewpoint,* during your lifetime you get the benefit of an income tax deduction for your charitable contribution and the assets are removed from your taxable gross estate before death. In addition, the assets you put into tax-free giving tools have the opportunity to appreciate in value, thus donating the current value and future appreciation. At the end of the day, the non-profits you support will receive more, and you'll pay less in taxes.

If you decide to make lifetime transfers, the earlier you start, the better. You don't need a large estate to make a difference. In the early stages of her career, Whitney became very active in the young leadership board for the Crohn's and Colitis Foundation. It was a wonderful way for her to learn more about her brother's disease and show her support for him. Frustrated by her lack of "liquidity" but eager to make a meaningful financial contribution, Whitney made a sizable endowment supported by a life insurance policy. Working with the legacy and endowment group, the Crohn's and Colitis Foundation was the owner and beneficiary of the policy. Each year when premiums were due on the policy, Whitney would make a charitable contribution to the organization which would in turn submit the payment to the insurance provider. Whitney received a charitable income tax deduction on the premium payments made and, since she was young and healthy, the premiums were affordable and the payoff to the Crohn's and Colitis Foundation would be substantial. Nothing could have prepared her for the qualitative benefits and deeper sense of connection with the community (and Ethan) after having taken this critical step.

The Importance of Planned Giving

Donors across the country engage in charitable giving every day. At first glance, smaller, more modest giving may seem inconsequential. While it's true that large amounts of philanthropy come from foundations and corporations, a deeper look illuminates the impressive impact of charitable giving by individuals. We all can make meaningful gifts that impact our communities or for causes that we care about. We all benefit from the qualitative benefits of giving and paying it forward.

For people with greater assets, the tax considerations may also help to increase charitable giving. Once your estate exceeds the federal exemption level, 40% of your assets above that level will go to federal estate taxes. This is in addition to any state estate taxes you may have to pay. However, any amount you decide to leave to non-profits upon your death comes off the top and passes outside of your taxable gross estate.

If your estate exceeds state and federal estate tax exemption levels, there are a number of strategic tools you can use to minimize the tax burden. I distinctly remember talking to a very successful woman who had a great passion for a number of causes, but charitable giving was not her primary goal when planning her estate. Her estate was going to be subject to both federal and state estate taxes. I pointed out to her that if she left her daughter her $1 million IRA, after paying federal and state level estate and income taxes, her daughter would only get a net amount of $300,000. In contrast, if her $1 million IRA was left to charity, the charity would receive the full $1 million. Suddenly she had a different perspective on how to plan her estate and charitable giving played a more integral role.

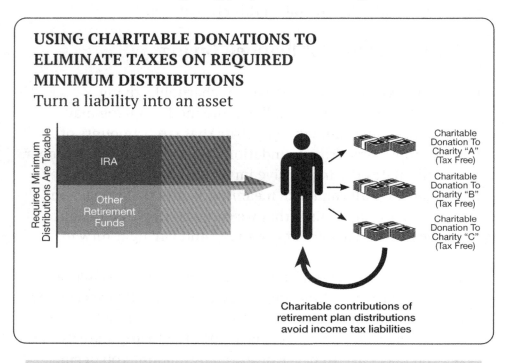

USING CHARITABLE DONATIONS TO ELIMINATE TAXES ON REQUIRED MINIMUM DISTRIBUTIONS

Turn a liability into an asset

Charitable contributions of retirement plan distributions avoid income tax liabilities

Donating Required Minimum Distributions during Your Lifetime

Generally, you are required to begin taking withdrawals from retirement funds, including IRAs, SEP IRAs, Simple IRAs or retirement accounts at age 70 1/2 (or upon reaching age 72 under the SECURE Act). However, a number of years ago, Congress made it allowable for individuals to direct distributions to non-profit organizations for up to $100,000 annually. If you take the required minimum distribution in a given year, you are required to report the tax on your income tax return. You could then make a charitable contribution and get a corresponding charitable deduction. In contrast, if you direct that $100,000 shall be distributed to a 501(c)(3) organization, you do not have to recognize the income. (You also do not get the benefit of the charitable deduction but, in some instances, the avoidance of the income tax translates into more income tax savings.)

— *Fund charitable gifts with appreciated stock* —

As an active philanthropist in the community, I regularly chat with donors on charitable giving. Over and over again I have heard donors get excited about the ability to get "miles" for charitable contributions made by paying with a credit card. But imagine trading miles for capital gains (or the avoidance of them!). Strategically used, charitable gifts can also help minimize capital gains taxes. If Jack and Diane wished to make a charitable donation, they could write a check for "cash" to the nonprofit. Alternatively, if they identify highly appreciated securities which could be donated, they could benefit from not only the charitable deduction but also by avoiding income taxes. Imagine they held Apple stock purchased at $50 but now worth $135 per share. If they sold the stock, they would have to pay capital gains tax on the appreciation. In contrast, if they transferred the appreciated stock to a charity (or a donor-advised fund discussed later in this chapter), the charity is not subject to income taxes. When the Apple stock was subsequently sold at $135, there was no capital gains taxes due. In addition, Jack and Diane received the benefit of the full charitable deduction at $135 per share, providing an exceptional tax planning advantage.

Charitable Lead and Charitable Remainder Trusts

As implied in their names, these two types of charitable trusts have opposite meanings. Both enable you to remove taxable assets from your estate by using them to fund non-taxable trusts while still leaving at least part of these assets to your designated heirs. They differ in how the funds are distributed to heirs versus charitable organizations and vice versa.

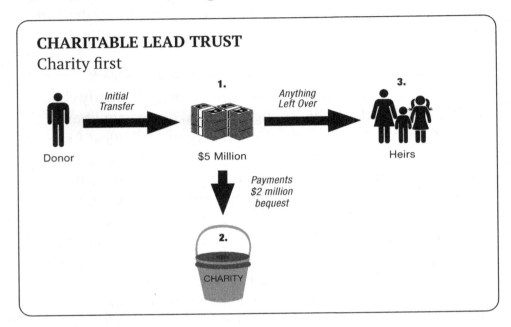

Charitable lead annuity trusts (CLATs) distribute funds to your designated 501(c)(3) organization(s). In other words, the charity "leads" the distributions and the remainder passes to your heirs upon the dissolution of the trust.

Charitable remainder annuity trusts (CRATs) take the opposite giving path. These trusts first distribute grants to designated non-profits. Upon the dissolution of the trust, the remaining assets are distributed to the designated charity.

New legislation surrounding retirement plan distribution requirements has also made CRATs increasingly popular. Under the prior laws, a beneficiary could "stretch" retirement plan assets over their life expectancy. However, under the SECURE

Act, which came into effect January 1, 2020, retirement plan assets cannot be "stretched" over the beneficiary's lifetime unless the beneficiary is an eligible designated beneficiary (like a spouse, a special needs beneficiary or a beneficiary who is within 10 years of the age of the decedent). Thus, in those instances where a beneficiary is an adult child, the retirement plan assets must be distributed from the IRA within 10 years. But planners have found that by making a CRAT the beneficiary of a taxable retirement plan account, we can indirectly get a "stretch benefit."

When a CRAT is the beneficiary of an IRA:
1. Upon death, distribution is made from IRA to CRAT (tax-free transfer).
2. The estate gets a partial income tax deduction equal to the present value of the remainder interest that is estimated to ultimately pass to the charity.
3. The annuity trust payments from the CRAT are taxable to the income beneficiaries of the trust but can be stretched over a

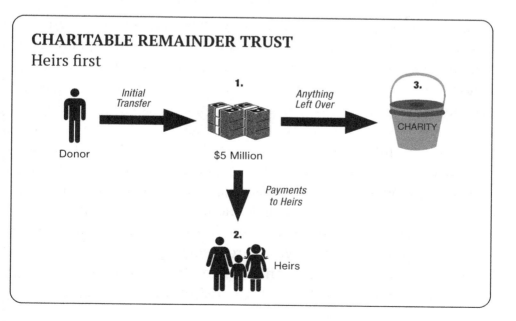

CHARITABLE REMAINDER TRUST
Heirs first

Donor → *Initial Transfer* → **1.** *$5 Million* → *Anything Left Over* → **3.** CHARITY

Payments to Heirs → **2.** *Heirs*

period of time longer than 10 years.

Essentially, by naming the CRAT as beneficiary, you are able to stretch retirement plan assets over a longer time period and the balance then passes to charity. Income taxes are deferred over a longer time period and charitable deductions are recognized.

Using Beneficiary-Named Assets as Charitable Tools

The two most overlooked assets in charitable estate giving are those with listed beneficiaries — retirement plan benefits and life insurance policies. Both of these beneficiary-designated tools help avoid probate, but the assets are still included in the decedent's taxable gross estate.

Life insurance policies are an incredibly easy-to-use tool since you do not need an attorney to create documentation. This tool was critical for Whitney, enabling her at a young age to leave a sizable endowment to her favored charity. Nonprofits don't have to be the owner of a life insurance policy used for gifting. The owner can be the beneficiary, and you can easily update the beneficiary designation on the policy to leave it directly to your favored charity or a donor-advised fund (discussed later in this chapter).

Retirement plans are, hands-down, the most tax efficient way to leave assets to a nonprofit. After your death, most of the assets owned by the decedent get a step up in basis to fair market value. A home built for $300,000 and now worth $1 million receives a step-up in basis to $1 million so that when the family sells the home, no capital gains are recognized. Unfortunately, the same is not true of retirement plan assets. Taxable retirement plan assets like 401(k)s, 403(b)s or traditional IRAs

BENEFICIARY-NAMED ASSETS AS CHARITABLE TOOL
Do good and decrease tax liabilities

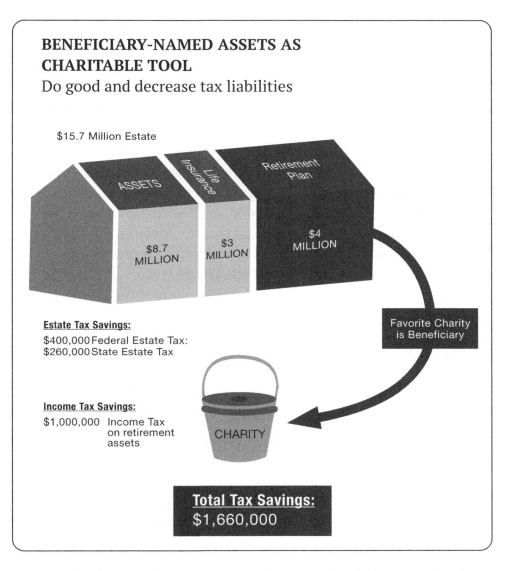

are still subject to income taxes after your death. You received a benefit during your lifetime by postponing the payment of taxes, but eventually, the income taxes are due. By leaving retirement plan assets directly to a non-profit, they transfer estate tax and income tax free, which can translate into more than a 70% tax savings.

If a specific bequest is included in your will or trust, the estate or trust would have to liquidate assets and then make a distribution to a charity. Instead of having a specific line item as a bequest in your will or trust, first allocate a percentage of your retirement plan directly to a non-profit or donor-advised fund that the next generation can take over. But, in the event you live a long and healthy life and spend down your retirement plan assets, you should have a savings clause in your trust to ensure that a specific amount of assets pass to charity. For example, your trust can provide that $50,000 shall be distributed to the American Cancer Society provided that such amount is reduced by any amount passing to the charity through a retirement plan beneficiary designation. Thus, if the charity received $35,000 from your IRA, the trust would only distribute an additional $15,000 (for a total of $50,000).

Private Family Foundations

For clients with significant assets interested in making meaningful charitable contributions, family foundations offer the greatest amount of flexibility and control.

Family foundations are set up as a separate corporate entity that applies for tax-exempt status with the IRS. They do require legal assistance with the initial set-up and maintenance.

The IRS requires a private family foundation to distribute at least 5% of its assets each year to public charities. In addition, there is annual maintenance with the secretary of state where the foundation is formed and with the IRS through a filing of a Form 990, which provides the public with financial information about the foundation. The overarching goal of these legal requirements is to help prevent organizations from abusing their tax-exempt status.

For families interested in making significant charitable contributions during their lifetimes or at death, family foundations are an extraordinary tool. Time and again they have proven to be a compelling planning tool to bring families together to engage in philanthropy and charitable grant making.

Donor-advised funds

A donor-advised fund (DAF) is a dedicated fund or account for charitable giving. DAFs were initially created in the early 1930s by the New York Community Trust and supported and sustained by John D. Rockefeller Jr. In 1991, Fidelity Investments became a DAF sponsor, becoming the first commercial DAF, helping to spur the growth and accessibility of DAFs.

Similar to a private foundation, the donor can select the name of the fund. Unlike a private foundation, there are no start-up costs, no ongoing legal or accounting fees, and no requirement to distribute a specific amount annually. Donors contribute cash, publicly traded stock or other assets to the DAF, and the cash or proceeds from the sale of assets are held in an account where they can be invested and earn interest. Then, fund holders or "donor advisors" recommend that the sponsoring organization, which maintains and operates the DAF, make grants to specific charities. The only requirement is that the funds must be distributed to an organization with 501(c)(3) public charity status.

As an added bonus, charitable giving is streamlined through simplified record keeping. DAFs have also increased in popularity due to the limits on charitable deductions. When filing personal federal income taxes, taxpayers have the option to use the standard deduction or to itemize deductions. No surprise taxpayers select the option that will reduce their overall tax liability. The Tax Cuts and Jobs Act (TCJA) practically doubled the standard deduction allowed but also placed limits on the amount a taxpayer can deduct for state and local taxes and property taxes. Because of the dramatic increase to the standard deduction, fewer taxpayers are expected to itemize their deductions.

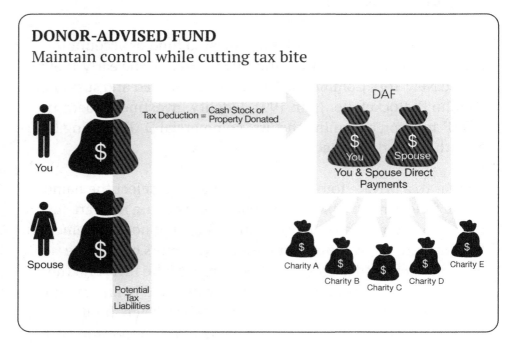

DONOR-ADVISED FUND
Maintain control while cutting tax bite

However, by donating more than usual to charity in a given year, taxpayers can exceed the standard deduction leading more of them to itemize their deductions. As a result, the TCJA has brought the concept of "bunching" charitable gifts to the center of countless tax planning conversations.

Bunching is a way to give more strategically and leverage your tax planning by grouping, or "bunching," a few years of charitable gifts in a given year. Essentially, you make a charitable gift large enough in the current year to itemize your charitable deductions. Then, over the next few years, you can simply make distributions from your DAF and get the tax benefit of the standard deduction ... and then continue alternating between itemizing deductions and using the standard deduction.

Consider Jack and Diane who could use a DAF set up for them by the Bernard Zell Endowment Fund to double or triple their charitable giving by bunching their donations. This year they could take itemized deductions and next year take the standard deduction ($25,100 in 2022) although they didn't make any direct charitable gifts outside of their estate. In the future they could direct assets from their DAF to be distributed to specified non-profits, including The ARTe Project, Chicago Institute of Art, the Crohn's and Colitis Foundation and the Advocate Children's Hospital, greatly increasing their charitable reach while improving their tax situation.

— *How to open a DAF*

Most broker dealers and wealth advisory firms offer DAFs. However, many are surprised to learn that nonprofits, such as National Philanthropic Trust and even local nonprofits such as the Jewish United Fund of Metropolitan Chicago (JUF), also sponsor DAF programs. In reality, charitable organizations were at the forefront of DAF planning. Many charitable organizations began their DAF programs well before many financial institutions started establishing separate not-for-profit wings in order to house donor-advised fund programs.

When choosing a DAF, consider the following:
- Minimum requirement to open a DAF
- Management fee(s)
- User-friendly portal to make grants
- Ability to name a successor advisor or advisors — or several

across generations
- Option to recommend investment management
- Accessibility to professionals in philanthropy

— *Creatively using a DAF*

Critics of DAFs express concerns that assets will accumulate in the fund and not be distributed to charity — my experience has been quite different. Even in instances where clients have allocated money to a DAF and elected to allow the fund to grow, they still make regular annual charitable contributions.

One family used its DAF as a tool to pass the donor-advisory role to one of their children. The couple has two successful adult children, David and John. John attained a level of success whereby he valued the ability to direct charitable assets. The couples' estate plan provides that the amount in the DAF at the time of the death of both parents would be treated as if it was an "advancement" or part of John's inheritance. Contemporaneously, John was appointed as the successor advisor over the DAF. The family discussed this idea and everyone agreed that the plan provided optimum planning for everyone in line with each beneficiary's respective goals and values.

Well-planned charitable giving will help you leave more of your assets to both build your legacy and support your heirs. It just takes some strategic thinking by a skilled professional estate planner to help guide you.

Conversation Starters
Fulfilling Your Charitable Wishes

When it comes to charitable giving, you need to think about your passions as well as your financial needs. Both play a role in successful estate planning because the more you save in taxes, the more assets you'll have to support the nonprofits near and dear to you. The better planned your support for these nonprofits, the more assets you'll be able to leave to your heirs.

1. **Have any nonprofit organizations really caught your attention? What kind of support do they need?**
    Before deciding to leave assets to charity, it is a good idea to know the kinds of nonprofits you would like to support.

2. **Do you want to leave something for them as part of your estate, or would you rather see things happen while you're alive?**
    This is always an estate planner's question. Know how important it is for you to see your money do good things.

3. **That stock we bought a few years ago is really going up fast. It could be a potential tax problem. Should you donate it to your favorite charity?**
    Why pay steep capital gains taxes on fast appreciating stock? Donating growing assets to charity puts more of your money to work on the things you care about.

4. **Are we sure the kids will be taken care of after we die?**
    Keep your priorities in mind. Charitable lead and charitable remainder trusts combine the needs of your favored nonprofits with those of your heirs.

5. **How important is it to you to leave something to your favorite charity?**
   Even if you don't have a lot of money to leave cherished nonprofits, there are ways to make a difference. Studies indicate that modest charitable contributions still make a lasting impact. And, depending on your age and health, purchasing a life insurance plan with a nonprofit as the owner and beneficiary is an excellent way to make a difference far beyond your financial means.

6. **Who is going to manage all this money we're leaving to charity?**
   Many nonprofits have ways to manage your endowment. You may also look into community foundations in your local area as they are excellent ways to match donors with nonprofits in need to support those things you are passionate about.

7. **We've earned a lot of money over the years, but is it really enough to save the world?**
   Together you can make a meaningful difference. Remember, a journey of a thousand miles begins with a single step. Take that first step and see how rewarding the journey can become, especially when others join you.

Chapter 13

Jack and Diane Get Divorced

After 42 years together and 35 years as a married couple, Jack and Diane ran out of words. There were no big, angry arguments. No embarrassing public incidents. No big affairs. They simply ran out of things to talk about. It was a slow process that, in hindsight, had taken a number of years. Both had built successful businesses, but had been growing apart even before Diane started her company.

Once they had felt an inseparable bond and considered themselves an unbreakable family unit. Both had a hard time remembering life without the other. After all, they were high school sweethearts. They raised three marvelous children, celebrated business successes, knew the joy of winning and the agony of losing. They shared memories no one else would ever understand. However, past memories don't necessarily dictate the future.

Somehow, they'd arrived at a place where they were no longer together. Quietly they'd gone their separate ways without even talking about their individual paths. Diane had built a new group of friends and business associates separate from the circles that Jack travelled in. Her interests had always been more home-based, even after Katie, Ethan and Whitney left the nest.

Jack, on the other hand, had seen his own social circles quietly grow in harmony with his business, now a global concern. He spent more time in airports and foreign cities than he did at their Fox River estate. He had increasingly been captivated by the politics of the areas where he did business, and found Diane had little interest in things that so deeply intrigued him.

Jack was no longer a necessary part of Diane's world and she didn't really understand his. Rather than continue on as two strangers occasionally sharing the same roof, they decided it was time each of them moved more solidly into their separate worlds, alone.

Why Every Divorced Couple Needs a New Estate Plan

Divorce changes the family unit. Each spouse may now form new relationships and families.

There are a number of ways to resolve a divorce to avoid divisive and costly litigation. Arbitration, mediation, and the most popular form as of late — collaborative law — offers couples the ability to end their marriage respectfully. Unfortunately, even in the most amicable of divorces, the process is stressful and filled with emotional, financial and legal complexities. Amidst this turmoil, many people fail to consider the estate planning and estate tax implications of their separation and divorce.

From an estate planning perspective, there are two distinct phases of divorce — the pending stage, and the stage when the marital settlement agreement is approved by the courts. While the divorce is pending, you are still considered to be legally married. As such, your spouse (or future ex) still stands to inherit if you do not survive the tumultuous divorce.

However, once a court approves the marital settlement agreement and the divorce decree is issued, everything changes. At this point you need to consider who you want your estate to care for in the future, guardianships for minor children and who you want to control your financial and health-related decisions moving forward. A new family dynamic requires some simple structural changes to your estate plan and a possible rethinking based on new financial realities.

Potential Problems While the Divorce is Pending

A divorce can take time. Depending on the level of contentiousness, it may take months, or even years, to equitably separate two lives. During this time, most states consider couples still married with full rights to marital property and any power of attorney rights granted before the divorce filing. Filing a petition for divorce is not enough. Even if a judgement is entered orally, it is not considered "final" until the signed order is approved by the court.

It may take months, or even years, to equitably separate two lives

---

When people realize how long the divorce process may take, they sometimes panic to learn their soon-to-be-ex has power of attorney over their financial and even their health decisions. The thought of a soon-to-be-ex having the authority to pull the plug gives nightmares to many people going through divorce.

Things can become even more muddled if one spouse dies while the divorce is pending. In most states the surviving spouse will be treated as if they were still married. Absent an estate plan, a surviving spouse living in a state like Illinois, would inherit 50% to 100% of the decedent's estate, depending on whether or not the decedent had children. If there was an existing estate plan in place, the terms would govern and likely identify the surviving spouse as the beneficiary.

An estate passed to a surviving spouse in this manner may eventually pass to people the deceased spouse never intended to benefit. Unless changes were made to that spouse's estate plan before they died, their hard-earned assets may well pass to the surviving spouse's family or even the surviving spouse's new family.

Most states have "statutory elective shares" for surviving spouses to help ensure that a spouse will not be disinherited. In other words, if a spouse is disinherited, she can file a claim against the estate to receive what the law will allow. But some states, like Illinois, look at the elective share of the estate (and not the trust). Thus, if you have all of your assets in a trust, a surviving spouse could potentially be disinherited because no assets will pass through the estate. Other states, like Florida, have complex statutory elective share calculations that take into consideration the estate, trust and even retirement plan assets. You need to consult with local counsel to see what your options are. And also consult with your divorce attorneys who can advise if the judge or opposing counsel is likely to inquire about changes to estate planning documents.

A To-Do List While the Divorce Is Pending

Remember that marriage is considered a partnership by law. If one spouse dies while a divorce is pending, with no prenuptial agreement in place, the law allows the surviving spouse to claim a minimum amount of property, often referred to as an "elective share." However, there are still a number of steps you can take during the pending phase of a divorce to change the flow of assets away from a soon-to-be-ex.

- **Change powers of attorney for property.** This is easily done even while a divorce is pending.

- **Update your power of attorney for health care or health care proxy.** The health care proxy allows you to name someone to make health care decisions for you. If, for example, you were in a car accident or had a health emergency and were unable to communicate, the person designated as your health care proxy would have the power to make decisions on your behalf. Unless you want your ex-spouse making these decisions — and most people don't — you need to name someone else you trust.

- **Update beneficiary designations.** Again, this is easily done even while a divorce is pending. However, be sure to cover all your bases. Insurance policies and retirement plans can easily be updated unless they are "qualified" plans governed by federal law and requiring spousal consent such as a 401(k). And some states take beneficiary designations into consideration for purposes of determining the elective share.

- **Revise asset plan.** Changing how assets are handled in your estate plan is not always easy or even possible. The goal is to ensure you maintain control of both beneficiary designations and tax advantages. For assets held in your individual name or in the name of a revocable living trust, planning can be very effective, providing it does not violate any court orders restricting transfers or revisions to estate planning documents.

Jointly held assets present more difficulty. When a married

couple jointly holds title to virtually all of their assets, they automatically pass to the surviving spouse by law, regardless of the terms of their will or trust.

Estate Planning Considerations during Divorce

A divorce is a negotiation leading to a new family dynamic. Your most basic concern will naturally be control of your assets and removing your ex-spouse from any future control over decisions affecting your life, estate and beneficiaries. In addition to the steps you should take to protect yourself while the divorce is pending, you should also keep the following in mind as your estate needs change to reflect your new family situation.

1. **Revise your will and trust.** Remove the provisions for your ex-spouse and make sure they are removed as the executor and trustee. You might also want to make sure that side of the family is also removed from such positions. You will probably want to make sure your ex does not receive any assets if you die and has no future control over your estate or trust. In the event your state does not allow you to disinherit a spouse through a trust, work with an attorney to have the documents ready for your signature immediately following the divorce.

2. **Rethink guardianship if you have minor children.** You may choose to name your ex-spouse as the guardian over any children in your will. Even if you don't, your ex-spouse will most likely serve as guardian of your minor children if you pass away unless they are determined by the court to be unfit. However, if your divorce is contentious or if your ex-spouse has a substance abuse problem, you may want to name someone other than your ex-spouse as the guardian to protect your children.

3. **Make sure you have a trust for minor children.** If you do not have such a trust, and your ex-spouse is the children's guardian, they will have control of the children's finances until they turn 18. Most clients do not want an ex-spouse potentially controlling their children's monies. To avoid this situation, you should have a revocable trust with your choice as trustee having the ability to access and control the money for your children if you die.

4. **Pay particular attention to life insurance requirements.** It is very common for marital settlement agreements to require a party to maintain a specific level of insurance coverage to ensure adequate funds for child support or maintenance/spousal support if one party dies. It is also common for the agreements to reference a trust without providing details around the specific terms of the trust in question. And, perhaps given the net worth of the couple, an irrevocable life insurance trust may be recommended. It is never too early to consult with an estate planning attorney. They can help avoid ambiguity in the agreement as it relates to trust requirements and ensure the agreed upon settlement meets your particular needs. Spending a little more time coordinating ownership and beneficiary designation through an irrevocable life insurance trust could potentially translate into millions of dollars of estate tax savings for the couple (and ultimately your children).

5. **Check your beneficiary designations.** Although most qualified plans (such as a 401(k)) require a spouse's signature to update beneficiary designations and list someone other than a spouse, consider updating the beneficiary on your IRA assets as soon as possible.

Things to Remember after the Divorce Agreement is Signed

At some point, probably later than you wanted, your divorce will be final and you'll take your first steps as part of a revised family unit. Now is the time to tie up those loose ends from your divorce and get your estate plan in order. Remove your ex from those old estate planning documents, take charge and get on with your life. At this point, here are a few final pieces of advice.

Tie up those loose ends from your divorce and get your estate plan in order

---

- **Consider the freedom of a name change.** For many, a name change represents the final act of closure. Take the initiative of owning your name and retitle assets into a trust which reflects the "new you."

- **Divide and retitle assets.** Thinking of selling the investment real estate that is currently owned jointly? What if it doesn't sell and one of you dies? Go through the exercise of recording a new deed to reflect the ownership as 50/50 instead of joint with rights of survivorship. While the marital settlement agreement can be used at a later date by family to enforce the agreement between the parties, who wants to create a situation that would potentially require litigation?

- **Update retirement plan beneficiary designations.** You may think you reviewed and updated them during the pending divorce — now is a critical time to review and update them again! Make sure your 401(k) and IRA beneficiary designations are updated to remove your former spouse. No matter what your estate plan or marital settlement agreement might provide, beneficiary designations govern. I have encountered several situations where folks never updated their beneficiary designations after their divorce and then died unexpectedly. This can result in unforeseen consequences and litigation to correct who the beneficiary should have been. Some states automatically allow for a divorced spouse to be removed as the beneficiary in these instances, but proving that to the financial institution administering the account can be costly and time consuming.

- **Give your divorce agreement to your estate planner.** Your estate planning attorney needs to know what obligations you have to your ex-spouse in the event of your death. For example, if your estate planning attorney knows there is a sliding scale of life insurance requirements as the children get older, they can draft mirror language in your trust to meet your agreed upon terms — but not give your ex too much!

- **Don't forget about prenuptial agreements the next time you say, "I do!"** No matter how collegial a divorce is, it can be a stressful and challenging exercise, especially if there was no prenuptial agreement in place. I am often surprised how soon some people get remarried after their divorce is finalized. Needless to say, if you are thinking about getting remarried, make sure you consult with an attorney to determine if a prenuptial agreement is recommended or risk traveling through the same divorce swamp again.

Collaborative Divorce Concerns

Some couples choose a friendlier divorce process that can avoid contentious litigation, minimize time, energy and attorney fees. These types of divorces, known as "collaborative," enable a couple to negotiate an acceptable divorce agreement with some professional help. In a collaborative divorce, all of the parties and attorneys sign an agreement that they plan to collaborate as part of the process. In this way, everyone comes to the table with the goal of a respectful and equitable division of assets and agreement regarding maintenance and child support. This is a phenomenal opportunity to think beyond the divorce to estate planning, gifting and wealth transfer considerations.

These are the things you should discuss with legal and financial professionals:

- Who should act as guardian if minor children are involved?
- What are the estate tax implications of the division of assets and life insurance policies?
- What specific terms should be considered to protect children from outside creditors and potentially bad decisions?
- At what age would you trust the children to become their own trustees?
- Does the couple wish to collaborate to create a cohesive gifting program for the strategic transfer of wealth to the children?

Fight "Attorney Fatigue"

After a divorce is complete, many people feel they need a break from attorneys. I understand. However, if you don't bother to update beneficiary designations and estate-planning documents, the courts will control many of the most critical issues with your estate.

Unlike divorce, the estate planning process is controlled by you. Should you fail to make necessary changes to your estate planning documents, the process could inadvertently become controlled by your ex or the court. With the right attorney, the process is incredibly easy and empowering.

Conversation Starters
As You Navigate a Divorce

Many divorces happen because people lose the ability to have meaningful conversations. However, in order to move on with your life after divorce, there are a number of things you should discuss with your soon to be ex, whether directly or through attorneys. There are also some conversations you might want to have with yourself as you move through the process.

1. **How are we going to afford two separate households?**
   Even the wealthiest among us still have a lifestyle they'd like to maintain. Dividing an estate often makes this more difficult, if not impossible. Having an accurate tally of your assets, income, debts and monthly financial needs will help you figure things out.

2. **What happens if one of us dies while the other still depends on support payments?**
   Insurance policies are often a good solution. Be sure your divorce decree outlines beneficiaries and responsibilities for maintaining a policy.

3. **Do I really want my ex-spouse controlling any of my financial or health-related decisions?**
   Even before your divorce is final, be sure to go over all power of attorney documents you may have in place. Those related to healthcare and financial instruments are critical to change.

4. **How do we make sure the kids are taken care of if something happens to one or both of us?**
   You will probably want to set up some form of guardianship arrangement in case you die or your ex-spouse is an unfit parent.

5. **Who gets my money if I die?**
   Divorce changes your family unit. Be sure to change all beneficiary designations on trusts, insurance policies and retirement accounts. Make decisions regarding real estate ownership and who will be the beneficiary of your other assets.

6. **What does our prenup say?**
   Too often this question never gets asked because no prenuptial agreement exists. These agreements really do make divorce easier to navigate. If you didn't sign one when you married the first time, don't make the same mistake again.

Chapter 14
Diane Meets Sam

Five years after her divorce from Jack was final, Diane went to visit her daughter, Whitney, now living in Boston and working as a book editor. Whitney was married to Jay, a whip-smart data scientist with the same ambitious outlook as her father. Their life was a bit of a whirlwind. So, while visiting one night, Diane decided to go out for a quiet evening. She stepped through the doors of a quaint little bar just a block from her downtown hotel, and there she met Sam.

Sam was very different from Jack. Although both had been high school athletes, Sam had actually enjoyed a career in professional sports, retiring at a young age and establishing a small downtown bar. By the time Diane walked through his door, Sam had been married and divorced himself with four children, one having become his business partner.

Sam wasn't looking for another relationship. Neither was Diane. But life happens, and Diane returned to Chicago only for the time it took to sell her downtown condo, pack up her things and move east. Fortunately, she and Sherry had sold their business the year before.

For just the second time in her life, Diane was starting a fresh new romance. Soon her long-time professional estate planning attorney flew to Boston, met Sam, and talked to them both about the families they were bringing into the marriage and their hopes and dreams for the future. This conversation led to a new estate plan for each of them that would help them realize their future and provide for the blended family. The circle of life keeps spinning.

New Estate Planning Concerns

According to data from the census bureau, approximately 17% of all divorced people remarry. Many others choose new life partners though they never marry. In other words, there is a decent chance the changes you made to your estate plan after divorce will need to be changed again in light of a whole new family dynamic. If you find yourself in this position, you may want to consider sitting down with your new spouse or partner and any children you both may have from previous relationships. The structure of their inheritance may well change and surprises often lead to bitterness and unnecessary legal fights when it comes time for them to inherit. Open communication and transparency can help avoid future conflict.

Most people entering a second (third or fourth) marriage bring assets, children and heirlooms into the partnership. If your intentions are to pass much of your estate to your children or give treasured possessions to certain family members, a revised estate plan is the only way to make sure your wishes are followed. As is true of everything related to estate planning, if you don't take care of it, the state will. And it will be messy and probably not handled in the way you wanted. You should now meet with your estate planning attorney to acknowledge and consider how you wish to provide for your new spouse and any step-children.

Ways to Protect Everyone's Interests

Second marriages often lead to conflicts between the concerns of new family members. You may have wanted to leave your home to your children, but your new spouse will need a place to live if you were to die first. One spouse may bring substantially more wealth to the marriage than the other partner. New relationships bring new responsibilities to care for each other and your new blended family. Working with your estate planning attorney, you can ensure your assets will pass in a manner consistent with the desires of you and your new spouse.

Certainly, a prenuptial agreement is as important in a second marriage as it was in the first. And after going through a divorce, individuals often have a different perspective and priorities. Perhaps they attribute even more value to the benefit of clearly laying out the division of assets to avoid unnecessary litigation. And often the parties in a second marriage are at a different point in their lives with significantly more individual non-marital assets. In my experience, the estate planning provisions in prenuptial agreements for second marriages prioritize the planning considerations at death just as much as those dealing with what would happen in the event of divorce.

Nonetheless, trusts are still incredibly important when it comes to developing your new estate plan. Trusts provide the best mechanism to control the flow of funds and ensure the assets left to benefit your new spouse will eventually pass to your children upon the death of your new spouse. No matter how loving they are, the surviving spouse may well move to another marriage, another blended family and another estate plan that leaves nothing to your children.

Basically, there are a variety of ways to develop an estate plan for a blended family. Each expresses a different vision of how you view your family moving forward. And as relationships strengthen and time goes on, your wishes may change. Over the course of your life, you can continue to make updates to your estate plan which reflect your wishes.

— All-for-one, one-for-all

In this vision, all children from both sides of the new family tree will be treated equally when the estate is passed on to them. After the death of both spouses, the estates will be distributed in equal shares to all children. Children from different spouses are treated exactly the same as those from the new marriage. For Diane and Sam, this would mean that after they both passed away, everything is divided equally amongst all seven of their children (Diane's three children and Sam's four children).

— Half to yours and half to mine

The assets of the new couple are divided equally between the two sides. These equal shares are then divided according to each spouse's wishes. Diane may leave part of her estate to a favored charity and divide the rest equally among her three children. Sam, on the other hand, may take his half of the estate and divide it equally among the four children from his previous marriage.

— What's mine is mine and what's yours is yours

A new estate plan designates assets to the side who originally brought them into the family. This may mean the assets Diane brought into the marriage will eventually pass to her intended beneficiaries, while those brought by Sam will pass to his own beneficiaries. In these circumstances, the parties often elect to keep assets separate during the marriage. The prenuptial agreement would provide that all assets will remain each other's individual non-marital assets during the marriage. For estate planning purposes, each party can waive their right to inheritance under one another's plans.

— *Our family is something else* ————————————————

Many new couples have a totally different view of how they would like to divide their estate. There may be a special needs child who requires a larger share to ensure their future care. Children of one or both spouses may be estranged from the family meaning they will be left out of any eventual distribution. Each spouse may also have special philanthropic desires they would like to see funded with part or all of their estate.

Some Basic Considerations

Every marriage, and family, is unique and demands personalization of their estate plan to meet their particular needs. The following are some of the most common situations you'll want to consider.

Providing for a new spouse with considerably fewer assets? In these cases, a QTIP trust (see Chapter 4) can be invaluable, allowing you to provide for a spouse who may survive you and subsequently pass to your children, while still allocating other assets to your children and other beneficiaries.

Marrying someone much younger. The younger spouse may be less wealthy as well. Often the children fear the younger spouse is just after the money, inviting family turmoil. This is especially true if the younger spouse is close in age to your children, causing them to fear they may never inherit. In these cases, you might consider leaving some assets to your children immediately upon your death, with the balance received after the death of your surviving spouse.

Controlling life insurance proceeds after your death. Too often one spouse passes away allowing the proceeds of an insurance policy to be distributed directly to individual beneficiaries. The proceeds can easily be eaten up by estate taxes, a spouse's irresponsible spending, skilled creditors, or predators looking to take advantage of vulnerable surviving spouses. Instead, it is usually wise to name a trust as the beneficiary allowing you to provide your spouse with lifetime income while maintaining control over the remaining proceeds.

Beneficiary designations take priority over the estate planning documents

Carefully consider retirement plan beneficiary designations. Remember that the beneficiary designations take priority over the estate planning documents. I have encountered countless scenarios where clients fail to update beneficiary designations — or fail to think through the potential implications. If a spouse, individually, is listed as the beneficiary of a retirement plan there may be income tax benefits by allowing the surviving spouse to "rollover" the IRA and treat it as if it is their own. However, this also opens the door to allow the surviving spouse to dictate control over what happens to the retirement plan assets on their subsequent death. Although the couple may have agreed to leave everything in equal shares to all of their children, the surviving spouse may elect to change the beneficiary on their retirement plan assets and disinherit step-children — or leave it all to the pool boy! Thoughtful planning can help ensure the assets flow through a trust and are held first for the surviving spouse and then pass in equal shares to the children.

Planning for disability and long-term care. If one spouse becomes ill and requires Medicaid assistance, the combined assets of both spouses will be considered "available assets," thereby increasing the odds that coverage is denied. In such cases, long-term care insurance will provide protection to both spouses. In other instances, more proactive planning is required in order to allow the surviving spouse to be eligible for Medicaid assistance.

To find the best solutions to all of these considerations, it helps to start with conversations between you and your new spouse. You might even want to include members of your new blended family. Then it's time to set up an appointment with your estate planning attorney and wealth advisor to make sure your financial and estate plans adequately reflect your personal needs.

Gifting and Estate Tax Considerations

As a married couple, regardless of whether assets are treated as individual non-marital property or marital property, you can make joint gifts or "split gifts." Consider that, by making a joint gift, Diane and Sam can together gift $32,000 each year to every one of their children. Through "split annual exclusion gifts," Diane can write a check for $32,000 to each child and take half as a split gift from Sam. Or, perhaps Sam has already gifted portions of his estate to his four children and, since his son now owns half of the business, he does not foresee needing to use his entire lifetime exemption. Diane and Sam can agree to make "split lifetime gifts" to Diane's children. If Sam does not need his entire exemption, he may be willing to let Diane use a portion of his lifetime exemption. Diane may wish to gift $2 million to her children but, by using a "split gift," she would use $1 million of her lifetime exemption and Sam would use $1 million of his lifetime exemption. This is often a concept which is negotiated as part of the prenuptial agreement.

Similarly, if Sam died prior to Diane and did not use his entire lifetime exemption, Diane could file an estate tax return to capture portability. By filing the estate tax return, Diane can capture Sam's unused exemption at the federal level and "port" it onto her return, thus increasing how much she could pass estate tax free upon her death.

Conversation Starters
A New Spouse

When you first married, you probably built an estate plan around the dreams of two people. After a second, third or fourth marriage, you will most likely be dealing with hard assets, multiple existing heirs and established philanthropic desires. Each family situation is unique, but here are some questions you should ask your new spouse before developing a new estate plan.

1. **What assets are you bringing into this marriage?**
    In the throes of a new love, you may not have thought about what you are both bringing into a new marriage. Is there a great disparity between your two estates? Is there disparity between current earnings — or potential earnings?

2. **What do your children already expect to inherit?**
    Have certain assets already been promised to one or more heirs? Perhaps one child has already been told that a favored heirloom will someday be theirs. Make sure old promises are kept and expectations managed.

3. **Is there anyone in our new family who will require special care after we are gone?**

   Children with special needs may require special considerations from your estate. Is there enough money in your estate to provide adequate care, or will a new life insurance policy be required to make up the difference?

4. **If something were to happen to me, would you likely remarry?**

   A surviving spouse who remarries, or enters into another relationship, could end up leaving the estate you left them to someone else's family. Estate planning can protect against those concerns.

5. **Do you have any creditors we should be aware of?**

   Current creditors are as troublesome as those you may acquire during your marriage. You'll want to make sure your new estate plan protects your assets. This will play an important role in ensuring that your estate benefits your intended beneficiaries (like family and charitable organizations) instead of the creditors of a beneficiary.

6. **Who do you trust to oversee your trusts?**

   Blended families do not require that all of the assets be "blended together" and be treated the same and controlled by the same trustee. Your new spouse may not feel comfortable using the same trustees as you used before and may envision a different division of wealth. However, blended families do require the couple to communicate their wishes and make certain their estate plan (including the titling of assets and beneficiary designations) reflects their goals.

7. **How do you think we should treat your kids and mine in our estate plan?**
   Are all children to be treated equal, or would it be better to treat them as separate branches of the new family tree? There is no right or wrong answer, just a reflection of how you view your estate and your new family dynamics.

8. **Do we want to both appear on the title of our house?**
   Remember that joint titling means the surviving spouse inherits the other's share of any assets. It also means the surviving spouse brings those assets to any future marriages or relationships, possibly disinheriting your children from assets purchased with your hard work.

9. **Would it be better to maintain separate estates?**
   By the time many people remarry, they are well-established with substantial estates. Many decide it is best to maintain separate assets and beneficiaries when they enter a new relationship. If so, start a healthy dialogue about a prenuptial agreement as soon as possible. This will help manage expectations and lay the foundation for open communication about financial and legal issues.

Chapter 15
Diane's Family Honors Her Life

It was the first Thanksgiving since Diane passed away. Don't be sad. She lived a rich full life from the time she left Iowa in the passenger seat of Jack's car until the day she died in her elegant Beacon Hill townhouse in Boston. She had enjoyed great love, the joy of parenthood, the pride of building successful businesses, the agony of divorce and the unbelievable thrill of finding new love in her later years. She had not left many stones unturned or dreams unmet. She lived to see her children become successful and her grandchildren graduate college. It was a good life.

Her children, Whitney, Ethan and Katie, gathered their families for another holiday together. Both their parents were gone now, as was Sam. They shared their grief at all they'd lost. Their memories of Diane were never far away, especially on that day. Deep into the night they remembered those special, life-long memories they held. That day when Whitney was surprised with her very first horse, a beautiful dappled gray Arabian. Ethan's first baseball glove and the train set that grew into a miniature city in a special room in the basement. Katie finally getting that trip to space camp she'd been leaving subtle hints for years about. And when Jack surprised them all with tickets for a trip to Disney.

No doubt they were lucky children to have successful parents whose hard work earned them so many beautiful memories. But it seems that both Jack and Diane had saved their best gift for last. A gift that could only be opened after their deaths — a well-planned estate.

The three children were well aware of the inheritance their parents had planned for them. They had received substantial gifts in the past as part of their parents' estate planning. However, the greatest gift turned out to be an orderly, sensible transition of wealth from one generation to the next, from one time to the future. A transition without rancor or judicial intervention. A transition that left the greatest portion of Jack and Diane's life's work to their family and treasured charities. A transition they never doubted being in line with their parents' wishes and family values.

Both Jack and Diane had a lifelong commitment to estate planning so their children could move on with their lives as quickly and comfortably as possible. Whitney, Ethan and Katie could not ask for anything more.

Things to Do after Someone Dies

Anytime a loved one dies, there are challenging days ahead — through the mourning process and administering the estate and trust. This list is designed to help you navigate the steps involved in bringing the wishes behind a carefully planned estate to life. This is not an all-encompassing list, but it's meant to provide a helpful overview. When you find yourself in this position, you must speak with an attorney to make sure you take every appropriate step.

File the will. Even in instances where you've taken the necessary steps to circumvent probate, most states require whomever is in possession of a will to file it within 30 days of death in the county where the decedent died.

If there is a trust, you will want to:
- Have the successor trustee formally sign an "acceptance" of the trustee role.
- Obtain a Federal Employer Identification Number (FEIN) for the trust. Although a Social Security number was likely used for a revocable living trust during life, a Social Security number dies with the person. At that point in time, a FEIN is required for the trust or estate...or sometimes both.

Notify Social Security. If a check from social security was received after someone's death, it is not uncommon for Social Security to take the money back.

Obtain death certificates. Request 20 death certificates. Although it is unlikely that you will need nearly that many, it is easy to get them upon death but can be time-consuming to obtain in the future. It is not uncommon for each financial institution or each insurance company to request an original death certificate.

Put together a list of all financial assets and liabilities. A professional CPA can help you review past income tax returns to make sure the list is complete.
- Assets:
  - » Owner
  - » Value as of date of death
  - » Beneficiary designation (if applicable)
- Liabilities:
  - » Debts
  - » Taxes
  - » Mortgage

Cancel credit cards. This may require a call to the credit card companies to determine if there are large outstanding balances. If so, try to negotiate a settlement. Be aware that sometimes a probate estate is opened for the sole purpose of trying to extinguish debt.

Retitle bank accounts and get step-up in basis to fair market value. Contact financial institutions to inform them of the person's death and request accounts be retitled to reflect the estate or trust. This requires the appropriate FEIN and signatory on the account to reflect the executor of the estate or trustee of a trust. The broker or financial institution should also update the tax basis on the newly titled account to reflect the value as of the decedent's date of death.

Confirm beneficiaries on IRAs and insurance policies. Work with financial institutions to set up a "spousal rollover IRA" or inherited IRAs. Confirm beneficiaries on life insurance by contacting insurance providers to claim funds and request Form 712, which your CPA will need to include in tax reporting.

Consolidate the assets of the decedent. While this may be a challenge, do the best you can.

Review real estate holdings to ensure probate avoidance and maintain insurance on property. Review all real estate holdings, including timeshare investments, which are often documented through a deed (instead of a simple legal contract). The physical location of the real estate plays a role in determining what steps are required to transfer and administer each property. While this is being examined, make certain the executor / trustee maintains the appropriate property and casualty insurance on the property. And even if no estate tax return is required and the beneficiaries plan to retain the property, get an appraisal on the broker opinion letter to document the value for purposes of step-up in basis.

Open a probate estate. If a probate estate is required, engage an attorney to assist and get the estate opened as soon as possible. Even in instances when a probate estate is not required, it sometimes makes sense to open one in order to start the creditor claims period as early as possible. In Illinois, for example, if a probate estate is opened, creditors have six months to file a claim. If no probate estate is opened, you run the risk a creditor could surface within two years of the decedent's death.

And, if probate is required, you will want to get the estate opened as soon as possible to obtain "letters of office" which would allow you to access and administer those assets.

File final income tax returns. If, for example, John Smith died on August 15, 2021, then:
- A final personal income tax return must be filed for the decedent from January 1, 2021, through August 15, 2021.
- A fiduciary return is necessary for the estate or trust (or sometimes both) from August 15, 2021, forward. If the estate or trust is administered quickly, often your CPA can file a first and final return. This fiduciary return must be filed any time income is generated of $600 or more, so it is a low threshold.

Determine if an estate tax return is required...or recommended to save millions in the future. If the decedent's assets plus lifetime gifts exceeded the exclusion amount at the federal or state level, an estate tax return is required to be filed. This return is due nine months from the decedent's date of death and the executor or trustee may also file for an extension to have an additional six months to file the estate tax return.

Imagine that Jack's estate was valued at $7 million as of his date of death and he made $8 million in lifetime gifts. The total value of his taxable gross estate would be $15 million. If he died in 2022, his exemption would be $12.06 million. Thus, he would owe estate tax at the federal level. If he lived in a state like Florida with no estate tax at the state level, no estate tax would be due to the state. But, if he remained an Illinois resident where the exemption is only $4 million, he would also have to file an estate tax return at the state level and pay the corresponding state level estate tax.

Recall that even if no return is required, you may need one to capture portability. In these instances, under IRS Notice 2012-21, the estate tax return must be filed no later than 15 months after the decedent's date of death. Because we don't know what the surviving spouse's net worth will be or what the tax exemptions will be in the future, filing an estate tax return to capture portability is strongly recommended as it could translate into millions of dollars of future estate tax savings.

Even if no return is required, you may need one to capture portability

If an estate tax return is required...so is IRS Form 8971. If the value of the decedent's estate plus lifetime gifts exceeded the exemption at the federal level, the executor is required to file an estate tax return (Form 706) and an informational basis return (Form 8971). On the filing, the executor is required to list the following:

- names of all beneficiaries receiving property from an estate

- beneficiaries' address
- beneficiaries' tax identification numbers
- the value (or new adjusted tax basis) in the underlying property for each asset

Look for beneficiaries and specific bequests. Review the decedent's will or trust to make sure these specific circumstances are taken into account.

Check with beneficiaries to make sure they all plan to accept the property and no one wishes to "disclaim." Those with a taxable gross estate who are the beneficiary of other assets can consider executing a disclaimer before accepting any assets. This has to be done within nine months of the decedent's death. The disclaimer treats the inheritance as if the beneficiary died before the decedent so the inheritance would then pass to whomever is next in line (like to children or a sibling if there are no children). It can be an incredibly efficient way to pass assets estate tax free if properly used.

Determine what you may have to provide beneficiaries. This may require a notice or some sort of accounting. Many states that have adopted the Uniform Trust Code and now require "notice" to be given to beneficiaries (often current and contingent beneficiaries) within a certain time period of the decedent's death.

Draft "receipts" to relinquish the executor or trustee from liability. This relates to the administration of the estate only. Receipts should be signed by anyone receiving property and it relinquishes the executor of any liability.

Obtain FEINs for sub-trusts. If Jack passed away and left assets in a marital or family trust or in trust for each child, different FEINs must be obtained for each trust (and separate income tax returns filed). Your attorney can help obtain the FEINS for you.

Check "unclaimed property" sites. This should be done for any and all states where the decedent lived to see if there is any unclaimed property.

Maintain records of expenses and distributions. Many expenses can be deductible on income tax returns filed for the estate or trust.

Determine how personal belongings will be divided. Look at the will and trusts for guidance and have a meeting of the minds of the family members. Set the stage for cordial and collaborative communication as soon as possible.

Maintain insurance and tax payments. These may include any property or casualty insurance owned by the decedent. You must also continue paying property taxes on any real estate they owned that will be inherited by others.

In the case of business ownership, update corporate records. This is done with the appropriate secretary of state office in the state(s) where the decedent held some degree of business ownership.

Review mail. You're looking for information to confirm assets and liabilities.

Obtain access to email and social media accounts. Immediately terminate any subscriptions. The Revised Uniform Fiduciary Access to Digital Assets Act (RUFADA), a law developed to provide fiduciaries with a legal path to manage the digital assets of deceased or incapacitated individuals, has been adopted by almost all states. This has helped people ensure their estate plan also covers their digital assets.

Conversation Starters
After Someone Dies

There are conversations you should consider having with aged parents, family members, or spouses who may ask you to help in administering their estates. The overall goal is to make sure their estate is handled as cleanly as possible and their wishes are fulfilled. Communication is critical.

1. **Who is their estate planning attorney, CPA, financial advisor and other professionals?**
   It's surprising how often someone forgets to pass on basic information such as this. The more you know about the professionals the decedent worked with, the smoother things will go.

2. **Are all of their beneficiary designations up to date?**
   It is critical for these things to be taken care of before a person dies. Remember that regardless of what an estate plan or marital settlement agreement provide, the beneficiary designations govern.

3. **What do you wish to see done with your estate?**
   Sometimes there are things in an estate plan that may be interpreted differently by different people. It helps to have a clear understanding in your own mind of the decedents wishes before the time comes to administer an estate.

4. **Are there any large debts?**

Surprises are never good. When Canadian publishing magnate Conrad Black mysteriously died, his lawyers were the ones to notify his wife and children that he was broke.

5. **Was everything the decedent wanted done with their estate plan done?**
   Sometimes new things happen that weren't yet accounted for in the estate plan. Will her daughter get the cocktail ring she just bought and mom promised to her? Did dad include that new charity whose board he recently joined in his estate plan or through a beneficiary designation on retirement plan assets?

6. **Will there be squabbles among the inheritors?**
   Sometimes family members have special items or personal belongings that they want. Do they actually inherit them? Can they just go take them or is there a procedure that must be followed? It's good to discuss any process with other actual or potential beneficiaries before things unexpectedly get out of hand.

CONCLUSION

Making a Difference Matters

Many people are surprised to learn that I did not start my career as an estate planner or even an attorney. I had a successful career in business and finance; a career that proved lucrative but not fulfilling. I wanted more.

I have always enjoyed working with people and helping them solve life's problems, large and small. I recognized that an attorney was involved in most critical decisions, and I wanted to learn more about the law. There I found my calling and passion.

Looking back, I see the difference my professional advice makes in the lives of so many families. As the daughter of successful parents and the mother of a little guy with a bright future, I see the value of a well-planned estate in a deeply personal way. The stories I could tell.

Here's one especially close to my heart. I've changed the names to respect privacy considerations, but it involves a family to whom I became especially close.

Harry, the crusty, caring family patriarch became like an uncle to me, and he sadly died before this book was finished. My relationship with Harry began on the other side of a legal matter with his daughter, Sarah. Sarah is a force in her own right, a successful career woman who consciously chose to become a single mother just a few short years before meeting Thomas, the love of her life. Thomas happened to be one of my clients, so when it came time for them to sign a prenuptial agreement, I was his attorney on the opposite side of the table from Sarah and her attorney.

Although we did not have any direct interaction in the prenuptial agreement negotiations, I was pleasantly surprised when years later Sarah referred her brother, Bill, to me when he needed estate planning advice. This work soon brought me into contact with their larger-than-life father, Harry.

Harry built a very successful business and had an air of confidence, competence and caring I always admired. For years he'd been told by CPAs, attorneys, business advisors and other professionals to do some advanced estate planning. Harry made small moves but often turned a deaf ear before making larger gifts. By the time I met him, he'd sold his business and become an even more successful investor. However, if he didn't quickly do additional advanced gifting, a large chunk of the estate he had worked to build was going to get eaten up by legal fees, probate expenses and taxes.

Looking back, I really don't know why Harry took my advice when he hadn't listened to others, but in the immortal words of Humphrey Bogart, it was "the start of a beautiful relationship."

Suffice it to say, when it came time for me to consciously become a single mother, Harry was one of the first people I told, and I relished his encouragement. One of my great memories was watching Harry hold my son for the first time.

Harry's death during the 2020 global pandemic was hard on everyone. His success in business was surpassed by his success as a father, grandfather, friend and philanthropist. Pandemic restrictions prevented us from visiting him before his death or gathering in his honor afterward. A short time later, his family gathered in the backyard of Sarah's home to review his estate.

As a result of our planning, Harry was able to leave an orderly estate that was distributed exactly the way he wanted. There was money for his children, grandchildren and favored charities. Instead of asking his children to take care of his longtime partner, he made a sizable bequest to her, enough to ensure her comfort for the rest of her life. Millions of dollars went to his designated beneficiaries rather than taxes. And those funds are asset protected from creditors and designed to pass estate tax free from generation to generation, creating a full and lasting legacy. This was my last gift to Harry and his family — a well-ordered estate that gave Harry a feeling of fulfillment and peace of mind in his later years and harmony and peace for his family after his death.

However, Harry's death didn't end my relationship with his family. Shortly after, Sarah called to tell me her son, Andrew, was turning 18. She asked if there were any special things we should do now that he was entering adulthood. While meeting with Andrew and Sarah to set up powers of attorney for him, I couldn't help but reflect on the long road I'd traveled with their family since first sitting on the opposite side of a legal negotiation with Sarah.

I can't emphasize enough the peace and tranquility I've seen people experience knowing their life's work will live on exactly the way they want

It has been my great honor to work with many multi-generational families over the years. A dynamic environment and changes in the law present new estate challenges. I can't emphasize enough the peace and tranquility I've seen people experience knowing their life's work will live on exactly the way they want. I've witnessed the gratitude of children and grandchildren after we've maximized a parent's legacy and given them a roadmap to fulfill their parent's wishes. I've also seen how a substantial bequest has enabled a client's favorite charity to make a meaningful difference in the lives of others.

We all come to crossroads in our life at one time or another. The fork in the road I followed led me to people like Harry and so many other extraordinary families I've had the pleasure of working with over the years. My gratitude is to them for helping bring meaning to my life. In return, I am honored to give them a gift for the future — an orderly estate that brings their legacy to future generations.

SECTION 3:

Impact of Residency on Estate Planning

Throughout this book I referenced how factors vary based on where someone lives. This section will detail, state-by-state, some of those factors, including whether or not there is a state estate tax and the threshold to avoid probate.

This information is accurate as of the date this book is published. Because state laws could change at any time, you'll want to a make sure you talk to an estate planning attorney for the most current information.

Chapter 16
Where You Live Matters in Estate Planning

One of the key factors guiding any estate plan is the state where you live. The existence of state estate and inheritance taxes, as well as exemption levels and thresholds to avoid probate, all depend on the laws and rules of the state considered your primary residence.

Sometimes issues arise when you move your primary home from one state to another. Trusts executed in one state will remain unchanged in another. However, sometimes language in a will or trust refers to applicable state laws. These instances need to be reviewed keeping the laws in your new state in mind. Although most states recognize documents from another state, there may be income tax or estate tax planning benefits to update your estate plan.

Different States Have Different State Estate Tax Liabilities

Depending on your state of primary residence, state estate taxes may or may not be a concern. Many states do not collect estate or inheritance taxes. Others set their own exemption levels, while others simply mirror federal exemption levels.

In those states where the state exemption level is lower than the federal exemption, only state estate taxes are collected from that level to the federal exemption level. Once the federal exemption level is reached, both state and federal estate taxes are collected, taking a real bite out of any large estate.

In those states with no state estate or inheritance taxes, you only have to worry about federal estate taxes which kick in above the current exemption level at the time of death. The exception to this rule is New York where state estate taxes are levied on the entire value of any estate exceeding the state estate tax exemption level.

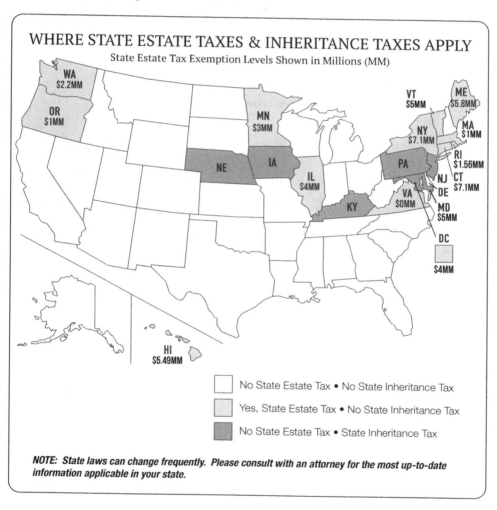

WHERE STATE ESTATE TAXES & INHERITANCE TAXES APPLY

State Estate Tax Exemption Levels Shown in Millions (MM)

WA $2.2MM
OR $1MM
MN $3MM
VT $5MM
ME $5.8MM
NY $7.1MM
MA $1MM
NE
IA
PA
RI $1.56MM
IL $4MM
VA $0MM
NJ
DE
CT $7.1MM
KY
MD $5MM
DC
$4MM
HI $5.49MM

☐ No State Estate Tax • No State Inheritance Tax

☐ Yes, State Estate Tax • No State Inheritance Tax

☐ No State Estate Tax • State Inheritance Tax

NOTE: State laws can change frequently. Please consult with an attorney for the most up-to-date information applicable in your state.

How Probate Rules Vary by State

Smaller estates may or may not be subject to probate. In Alabama, any gross estate valued at more than $25,000 must go through probate with all its associated hassles and costs. In Illinois, however, only those estates valued above $100,000 need to file for probate. In Wyoming, estates below $200,000 in total value do not have to go through probate court.

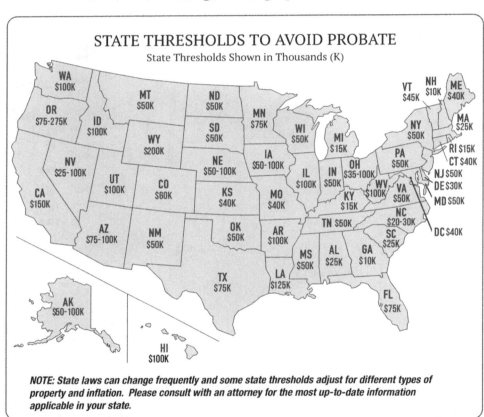

STATE THRESHOLDS TO AVOID PROBATE
State Thresholds Shown in Thousands (K)

WA $100K
OR $75-275K
ID $100K
MT $50K
ND $50K
MN $75K
VT $45K
NH $10K
ME $40K
NY $50K
MA $25K
NV $25-100K
UT $100K
WY $200K
SD $50K
WI $50K
MI $15K
PA $50K
RI $15K
CT $40K
CA $150K
CO $60K
NE $50-100K
IA $50-100K
IL $100K
IN $50K
OH $35-100K
WV $100K
VA $50K
NJ $50K
DE $30K
MD $50K
KS $40K
MO $40K
KY $15K
NC $20-30K
DC $40K
AZ $75-100K
NM $50K
OK $50K
AR $100K
TN $50K
SC $25K
MS $50K
AL $25K
GA $10K
TX $75K
LA $125K
FL $75K
AK $50-100K
HI $100K

NOTE: State laws can change frequently and some state thresholds adjust for different types of property and inflation. Please consult with an attorney for the most up-to-date information applicable in your state.

Remember, one of the primary goals of any good estate plan is to minimize or eliminate probate hassles. However, in low probate states, a necessary checking account or even an automobile not titled to your trust may tie up parts of your estate in costly probate.

Here are the thresholds to avoid probate court in each state. However, many states have varying thresholds based on property types and beneficiary relationships to the decedent while others annually adjust thresholds to keep pace with inflation. Please consult an attorney for specific information applicable to your state.

Property Ownership Can Change across State Lines

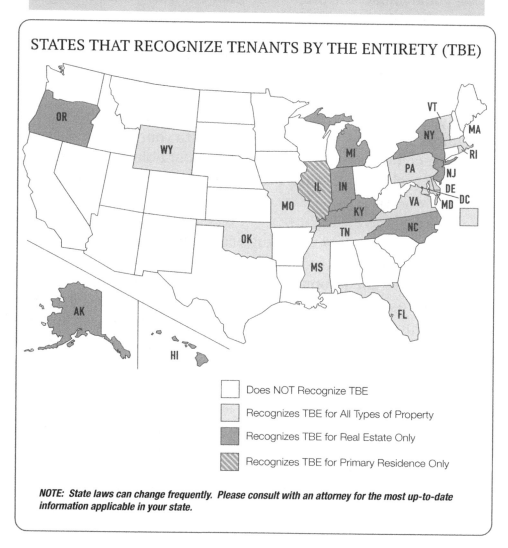

STATES THAT RECOGNIZE TENANTS BY THE ENTIRETY (TBE)

Does NOT Recognize TBE

Recognizes TBE for All Types of Property

Recognizes TBE for Real Estate Only

Recognizes TBE for Primary Residence Only

NOTE: State laws can change frequently. Please consult with an attorney for the most up-to-date information applicable in your state.

Another potential problem is how different states view property ownership rules. If your estate plan was written in a state that recognizes tenants by the entirety (see prior page), but your new state does not, it may affect the value of property in your trusts. In fact, it may alter the eligibility of certain properties to be included in your trusts. If your new state does not recognize tenants by the entirety, then you and your spouse may have to revise trust documents to reflect co-ownership arrangements that could impact the property in your trust, as well as future estate tax obligations.

Moving Between Community and Non-Community Property States

How your property is owned controls how safe it is from creditors, as well as how it can be passed to your beneficiaries. When it comes to community property, your home state when you first took control of the property casts a strong influence on future ownership.

If you bought property considered community property in California and moved to Illinois, a common law state, the property does not automatically change to separate ownership. Rather, it remains community property, even if exchanged, sold or replaced. However, if property, such as an investment portfolio, acquired in a community property state moves with you to a common law state, the ownership is separated with each spouse maintaining a one-half interest.

The rules are a little different when you acquire property while living in a common law state before moving to a community property state. Property obtained in a common law state that would be considered community property in another state becomes "quasi-community property" and may be treated as community property when a couple divorces or one spouse dies. This means that property previously owned by one spouse is no longer protected from creditor actions against the other. The solution, of course, lies in the proper use of trusts for your estate planning.

Use the chart below to find if your state, or the state you're moving to, is a community property or common law state, or if it allows for community property selection through trusts or other planning tools.

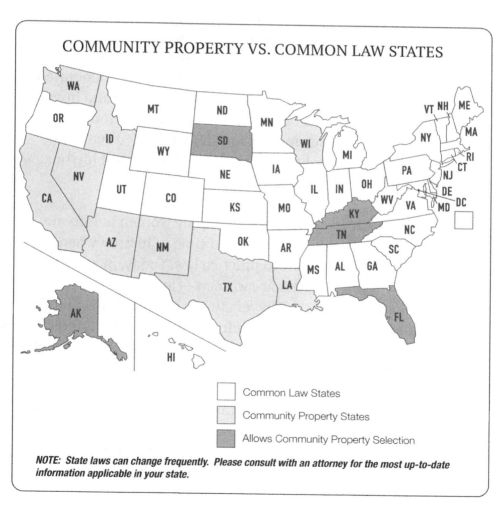

COMMUNITY PROPERTY VS. COMMON LAW STATES

☐ Common Law States

☐ Community Property States

☐ Allows Community Property Selection

NOTE: *State laws can change frequently. Please consult with an attorney for the most up-to-date information applicable in your state.*

Acknowledgements

I am forever grateful to my friends, family and strangers who helped pave a path for me to practice law. They say "it takes a village," but I have been blessed to see the impact of an extraordinary army of love and support help shape who I am.

There is no question that my parents have played a fundamental role in my development and success. They believed in me, and encouraged me to hone my skills — in academics and theater — to make a difference in my profession and the world at large. My brothers challenged me to compete with the boys — and encouraged my development. Family who are friends, and friends who are truly family, always celebrated my success. But far more important than the cheers and hugs in victory, when setbacks occurred, they supported and encouraged me to persevere. Because let's face it - the wrong turns and disappointments provided the most critical lessons for success.

In that vein, the fearless efforts of so many women before me are not taken for granted. There was a time in history when women were not deemed fit to practice law. Today, more than 50% of law school graduates are women — and women make up more than one-third of the lawyers in the U.S. I proudly stand on the shoulders of generations before me who have suffered and fought for diversity and inclusion so that I could participate productively in the greater legal community.

There were special mentors and strategic partners who held out their hands to teach and guide me in the practice of law and the art of the business. The all women networking groups of soul sisters illuminated me on this in practice long before it was a popular meme:

> "Another woman doing what you're doing is not
> your competition, she is your sister! Support her.
> Encourage her. Believe in her."

There were also many extraordinary men who saw me as an equal, recognized my ability to add new perspective and creativity to the discussions, and welcomed my collaboration. My army today consists of many remarkable individuals who come together to execute on my personal and professional visions. My "work family" is just that — a team of individuals at all levels of the organization who work tirelessly to service my clients. My network of personal advisors keeps me sane — and my team of caretakers who nurture my child with love and affection — allow me to do it all.

Above all, I am forever indebted to the clients who have entrusted me with their lives, their assets and their family secrets to create a gift for the future.